Thanks to

All Askan See, Nina Bacus, Craig Barrowman, Jimmy Furneaux, Fiona Gallacher, Nackt Insekten, Kevin Jamieson, John (from Aberdeen Market), Marcobe, Mark and David McCracken, Eva Merz, The Jan Van Eyck Academy, Jo Muir, Julie Peeters, Brian Ross, Donnie Ross, Nuno Sacramento, Pete Stollery, Bill Thompson, Transition Extreme, The Vacuum Cleaner, all shopkeepers and stallholders who shared their knowledge and opinions, and especially Graeme Cheyne.

ADAPTATION
Redesigning the everyday.

It's OK working everyday

I'm having some problems with my everyday life. I can't seem to locate it very satisfactorily. It's slippery and shapeless and I can't get any help from anyone else by comparing notes or experiences because we don't seem to have anything in common. I'm beginning to doubt that it's even here at all and the fragments I can grasp don't stand up to scrutiny. It's rife with gaps and flaws inviting interventions, modifications and revisions. It struck me that it is these invitations that call for a direct and critical engagement with a world that has been designed and built around us, an engagement that infuses a daily creative and political practice.

It is perhaps interesting to reflect upon the nature in which design infuses the day-to-day and some of the areas identified by artists for intervention. Social and cultural debate of what constitutes everyday life set against discussion around creativity and design's function in urban experience and development will hopefully provide a context to discuss possible approaches to the areas where the constructed world lets us down.

It's a convenient arrangement that the stage is set for the everyday. The famous designation of everyday life as 'what remains after one has eliminated all specialised activity'[1] by French sociologist and intellectual Henri Lefebvre emerged from a body of writing that has proved a key source for current readings of the notion of the everyday. When we contend with the world on a daily basis the specialised activity of design has already happened, initiated and delivered by someone else and now invisible and available for us in the shape of public transport, street furniture and signage, vending machines and coffee kiosks. In a world so seamlessly designed and furnished with products that just seem to have always been there or at least arrived without incident, it is easy to simply slot into the conveyor belt of the day-to-day oblivious to the fastidiously assembled world around us. It is this invisibility or at least lack of seams that so impressively reflects the specialisation involved in the construction of urban space. The theatre that the city provides for the everyday is a meticulous and complex one.

Pithy as Lefebvre's definition appears, I can't help feeling like I need a more comprehensive explanation of what constitutes the everyday and for such a perennially contested issue, that seems difficult to find. Most famously from its formation in 1957 the radical group Situationist International [SI] identified everyday life as a crucial terrain to address their revolutionary agenda. The SI viewed the alienation they judged to be the direct product of the post-war surge of advanced capitalism as inextricably bound up in the routines and processes of daily experience. Borrowing from Lefebvre's premise they offer little in terms of clarification, but interestingly this looseness can perhaps be reconciled with a fundamental commitment to experimentation and play. In 1967 SI member Raoul Vaneigem, wrote 'the true game and the revolution of everyday life are one'[2]. That there should be a certain plasticity to the manner in which the city is used and experienced is an exciting notion and one that is certainly at odds with the drudgery of routine or the myopic pursuit of profit. During their most active period from the late 50s to the early 70s the Situationists presented much discussion around strategies that might facilitate the re-examination of the use of city spaces via oblique cartographies, psychogeography - a discipline devised to study the impact of the geographical landscape on emotion and behaviour - and dérive - 'a mode of experimental behaviour linked to the conditions of urban society'[3].

Writer and curator Will Bradley presents a contemporary critique of the everyday. It is his view that 'the everyday remains mostly as something constructed by advertising and the media; privatised individuals consume the fantasy of everyday life'[4]. He debunks the Situationist project via the reflection that there is no sense that everyday life is a uniform experience. By virtue of your placement in culture and society the notion of the everyday will be marketed to you differently. There are only representations of the everyday no concrete thing-in-itself to be isolated for criticism. On the fact that this is so integrated into our experience, Bradley notes '[everyday life has] already been theatricalised by its depiction in mass media, and nowadays the process is so entrenched it feels almost redundant to point it out'.

For all that the Situationist model is flawed and in many ways outmoded, I find certain elements of their approach useful tools in comprehending and inspiring the conditions that invite the intervention and refining of the civic structures of the day-to-day. With Will Bradley's insightful revisions of what is constituted by the everyday we are equipped with a more innately mutable model whose illusive nature betrays the more insidious role capitalism plays in constructing our daily experience back here in the 21st century. I would venture that Vaneigem's game is still there to play, only, as often happens when players tire or grow dissatisfied with an earlier version, advanced and complicated.

In 1987 a gold-plated scale replica of the flame carried in the hand of the Statue of Liberty was installed at the north end of the Pont de l'Alma in Paris. Ten years later, after the death of Diana, Princess of Wales, in the road tunnel beneath it, the monument was gradually appropriated by mourners adorning it with tributes. Swiss sculptor Thomas Hirschhorn identified the Flame of Liberty as a key influence on his series titled *Sculptures Directes*. In his text 'Four Statements' he examines ubiquitous, near invisible civic structures such as roadside memorials, concession kiosks and public monuments and how they are utilised by an audience. His particular interest in the example at the Pont de l'Alma has nothing to do with the dead princess, but rather with the interface between the provision of civic sculpture for the public good and a direct engagement by the public itself changing its meaning to better serve their interests. He writes: 'What counts for me is that this sculpture is appropriated by its environment, signed, marked, changed and no longer imposed by a force from above, but integrated, welcomed or not welcomed, confronted by the heart, from below'.[5] Though probably not the design of this case in Paris, it offers an incisive critique of the demagogy inherent in much of civic public provision. It illustrates that in a strategically selected context elements of the city can be modified to serve the individual unpicking of the dominant force's complacent gesture to placate the masses.

Though the impact of the borrowing of the Flame of Liberty by the Parisian mourners is clear, it could be argued that such an example really just illustrates another media generated event, a mass hysteria even. This invites questions about the roles of individual artists or small groups of collaborators who hope to engage with the city, changing it to reflect their concerns or political perspectives. There are, of course, many precedents of creative approaches to modifying urban space. At about the same point the SI was dissolved, the newly increased availability of spray paint and indelible markers catalysed an explosion of graffiti writing on the North American East Coast. The disregard of authority at the root of the blooming graffiti scene can be viewed as a crucial fundament in the lineage of artists exploring the possibilities for using the city. Aside from undoubted radical aesthetic qualities, graffiti, in its most fundamental state as the tag, provides a whole additional network to approach the city. As a kind of cartography of civil disobedience, albeit one that might often require a certain degree of insider knowledge to read, there are traces and records of motion through a city, negotiations of authority and feats of daredevil bravado. It is easy to imagine that in the early '70s the Philadelphia streets and New York subway trains would have seemed like a pristine blank canvas much as Paris must have seemed one for serving the Situationist demands of the imagination, creativity, desire and pleasure.

Though the graffiti scene clearly ticks on, there seems to be little scope for innovation, content as it apparently is to cling to its somewhat staid roots. For those contemporary artists working with urban space who have not been incorporated into the institutions of public art provision and are eager to explore the possibilities for modifying their surroundings the terrain is uneven. For those who are keen to make incisive revisions city space must seem very far from a blank canvas. That is not to suggest that the possibilities for interesting interventions are limited, rather that the city presents a dense and textured mesh of experience. The topography of the everyday interlaces elements in profusion and in such an active way that it becomes amorphous. There is no sense that a large public sculpture will speak in a relevant way to every user of city space and audiences are varied and protean. The astute artist will not be perturbed and instead realise that in exchange it is this very topography that provides the tools, similarly varied and protean, for successful intervention.

Though the evasive nature of the everyday and its insidious exponents in the market place can prove an exciting and fruitful context to work, artists can find it difficult to situate themselves convincingly outside it all as spectators on its complexity. Indeed, commentators on the role of what is often alarmingly termed the 'creative industries' in the city will often identify the communities that surround and house practitioners in art and design as crucial factors in the way such cities are represented. The consequent link between urban clusterings of artists and economic growth is also reflected in the marketing of cities as progressive and tolerant, represented in the light of their creative communities. In happy alignment with our current perspective on the everyday economic and social, geographer Stefan Krätke acknowledges the role of creative communities as vital in the production of 'lifestyle images' and with them the marketability of urban centres. He states 'In virtually all branches of the economy, "market success" today is based largely on the construction of images and their communication to the media'[6].

Embroiled as we clearly are in all this, there is of course potential for disruption. We can see how the marketed image of the city can be countered by new strategies for representation through the sustained development of an archive of images categorising urban space that privilege the roaming subjective eye. Similarly the poverty of the uniformity of city furniture or temporary functional structures can be infused with narrative or be anthropomorphised through subtle and witty additions. The voices of those communities less valued by the indifferent economic visionaries such as small businesses and trades-people can be brought to the fore. Even the structures of authority provide pliable and potent media. One need only assume the guise of a construction worker or a city official with the donning of a high visibility tabard before the civic infrastructure becomes suddenly accessible and the contradictions of the public and private in the day-to-day can be explored. The by-products of the apparent efficiency of everyday life in the city can be collected and reinterpreted to expose the complacent lack of sustainability.

And graffiti, of course, is still fair game with its success lying in an acknowledgement of its scope once unpacked and expanded. Its clandestine nature can be brazenly exposed once documentation of inventive interaction with those areas normally off limits is bill postered across the city. The vocabulary need not be restricted to esoteric pseudonyms or near illegible, elaborate tags. There is potential for the uniformity of mechanically produced texts that appear alarmingly authoritative and fragments of overheard scraps of dialogue collected from the city. The palate need not exclusively include spray paint, magic markers and postage stickers when sewing kits are provided encouraging audience participation in mapping their own personal routes through the city. The role of the enigmatic, shadowy graffiti daredevil armed with industrial, masculine tools can be demystified to encourage all to partake with wry humour, equipped with the traditional tools of the unliberated woman at home.

There is a lot at stake in the city. It seems that efforts to refine or unpack the issues and content are somewhat futile as each interpretive gesture obscures or exposes another. With market places, economies and representations so deeply infused in daily interaction with urban space, a direct and experimental engagement with it might be the only way to avoid alienation and frustration. It strikes me that now, upon reflection, I'm coming to terms with the absence of the everyday, or at least the absence of one that I can share with others. It has become a fearsome armoury for examining itself, highlighting iniquity, exposing oppression, for play, imagination, desire and pleasure.

[Giles Bailey]

[1] Lefebvre, Henri, Critique of Everyday Life, London, 1991
[2] Vaneigem, Raoul, The Revolution of Everyday Life, translated by Donald Nicholson-Smith, Rebel Press, London, 1981
[3] Andreotti and Costa, Theory of the Dérive and other situationist writings on the city, Museu d'Art Contemporani de Barcelona, Barcelona, 1996
[4] Bradley, Will, 'The decline of the circus and the marching band is permanent and final', Afterall - A Journal of Art, Context and Enquiry, Issue 5, Central Saint Martins College of Art and Design, London, 2002
[5] Hirschhorn, Thomas, 'Four Statements, February 2000' in Public Art: A Reader, ed. Florian Matzner, Hatje Cantz, Ostfildern, 2004
[6] Krätke, Stefan, 'Global Media Cities in a Worldwide Urban Network', Research bulletin, European Planning Studies II, Routledge, 2003

ADAMS

SLUSSEN

Sluss is the Swedish word for passage. Slussen is a place in Stockholm where the city gathers, a traffic hub where north meets with south. It's a crossroads and a meeting place.
In this location, there's a small clandestine hut squatted on the sidewalk. Inside you find a hatch in the floor that opens to a tunnel network that takes you down and around. This clandestine hut is also called Slussen, it gives passage between the below and above.

STOCKHOLM VATTEN

Stockholm is often referred to as Venice of the North, water frames the commercial image of the city. Beneath the ground lies a network of hidden water pipelines. Rainwater, wastewater, sewer. A collapsible canoe makes these underground wells accessible.

TAKING PLACE - OWNING SPACE

The Stockholm Public Library holds around 500,000 books. Nine of these are hollow, placed there without any notion from the librarians. Each book holds a key and a map indicating its lock. They are part of a lending system which provides access to landscapes beyond the spectacle, free of charge and accessible to the public. A public service for public space.

[Adams]

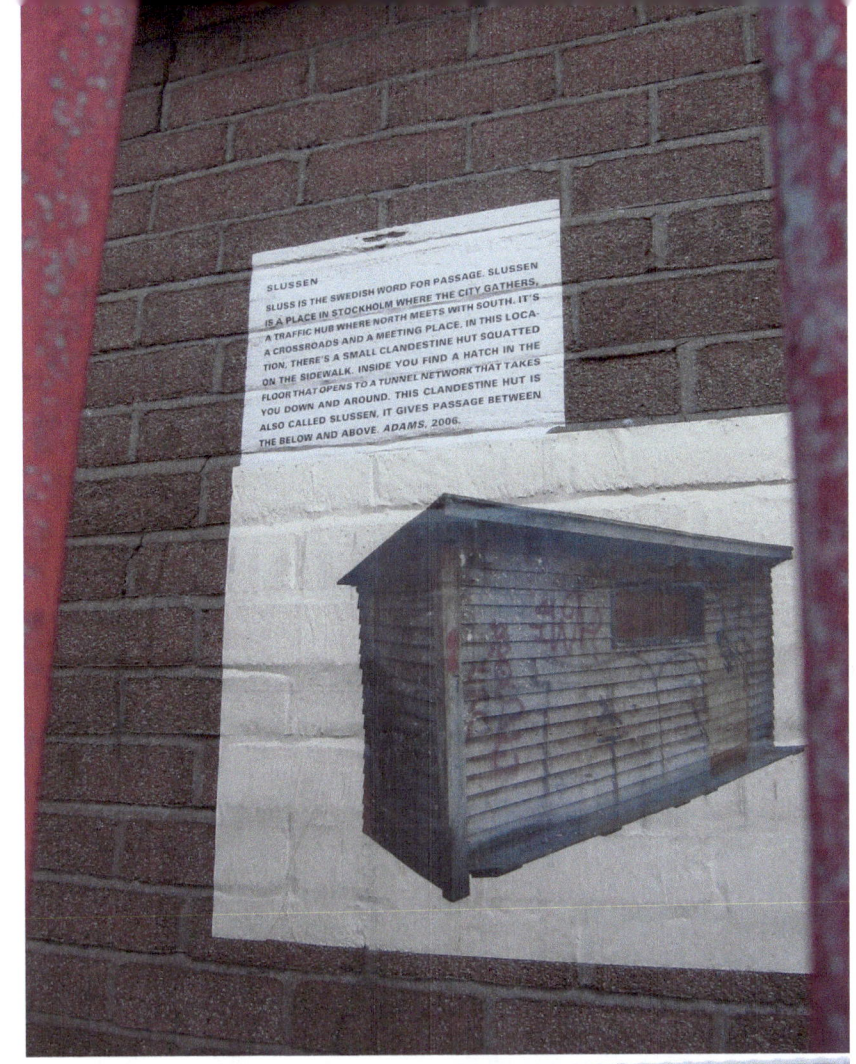

SLUSSEN

SLUSS IS THE SWEDISH WORD FOR PASSAGE. SLUSSEN IS A PLACE IN STOCKHOLM WHERE THE CITY GATHERS, A TRAFFIC HUB WHERE NORTH MEETS WITH SOUTH. IT'S A CROSSROADS AND A MEETING PLACE. IN THIS LOCATION, THERE'S A SMALL CLANDESTINE HUT SQUATTED ON THE SIDEWALK. INSIDE YOU FIND A HATCH IN THE FLOOR THAT OPENS TO A TUNNEL NETWORK THAT TAKES YOU DOWN AND AROUND. THIS CLANDESTINE HUT IS ALSO CALLED SLUSSEN, IT GIVES PASSAGE BETWEEN THE BELOW AND ABOVE. ADAMS, 2006.

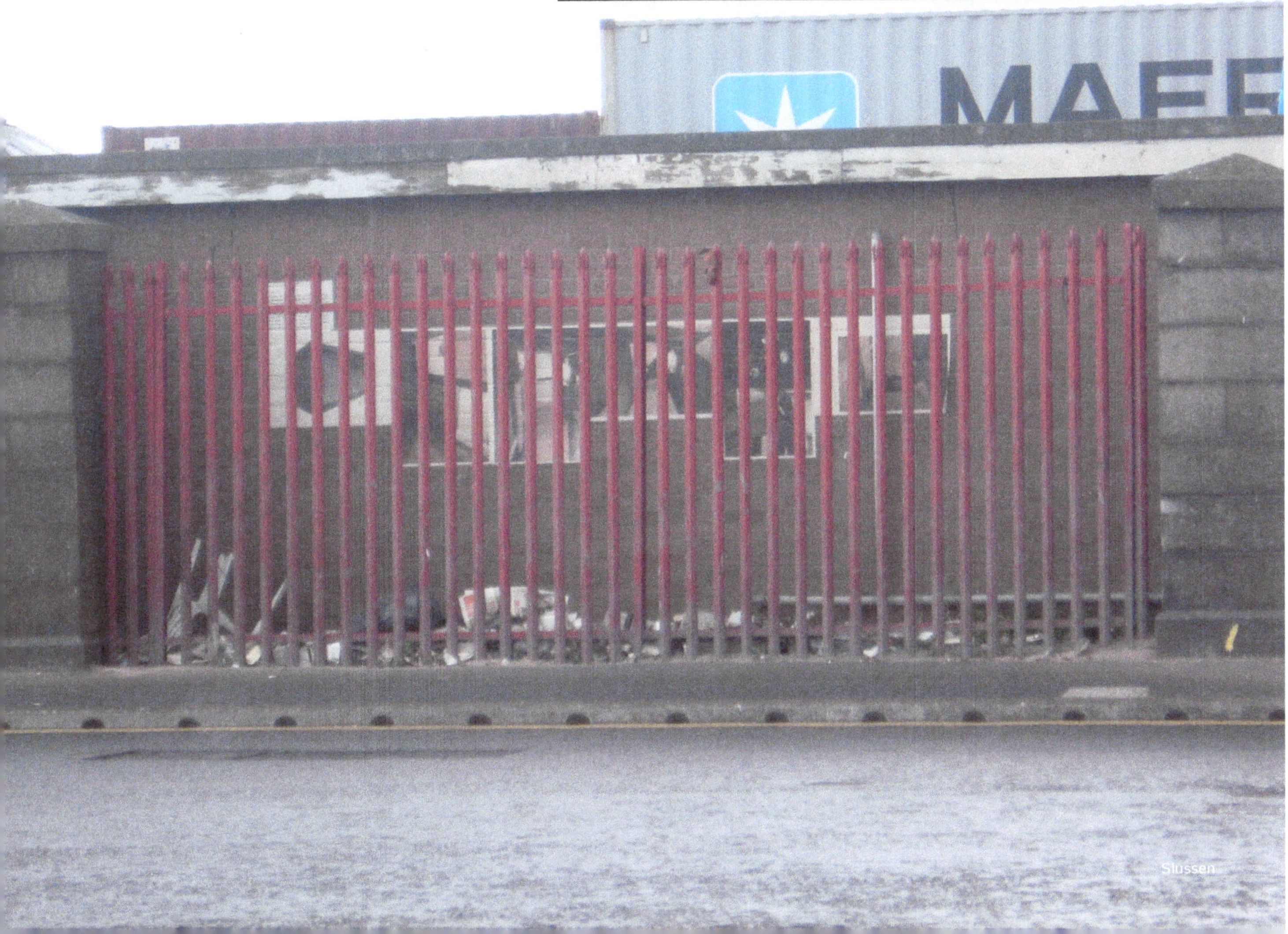

Slussen

STOCKHOLM VATTEN

STOCKHOLM IS OFTEN REFERRED TO AS VENICE OF THE NORTH. WATER FRAMES THE COMMERCIAL IMAGE OF THE CITY. BENEATH THE GROUND LIES A NETWORK OF HIDDEN WATER PIPELINES. RAINWATER, WASTE-WATER, SEWER. A COLLAPSIBLE CANOE MAKES THESE UNDERGROUND WELLS ACCESSIBLE. ADAMS, 2006.

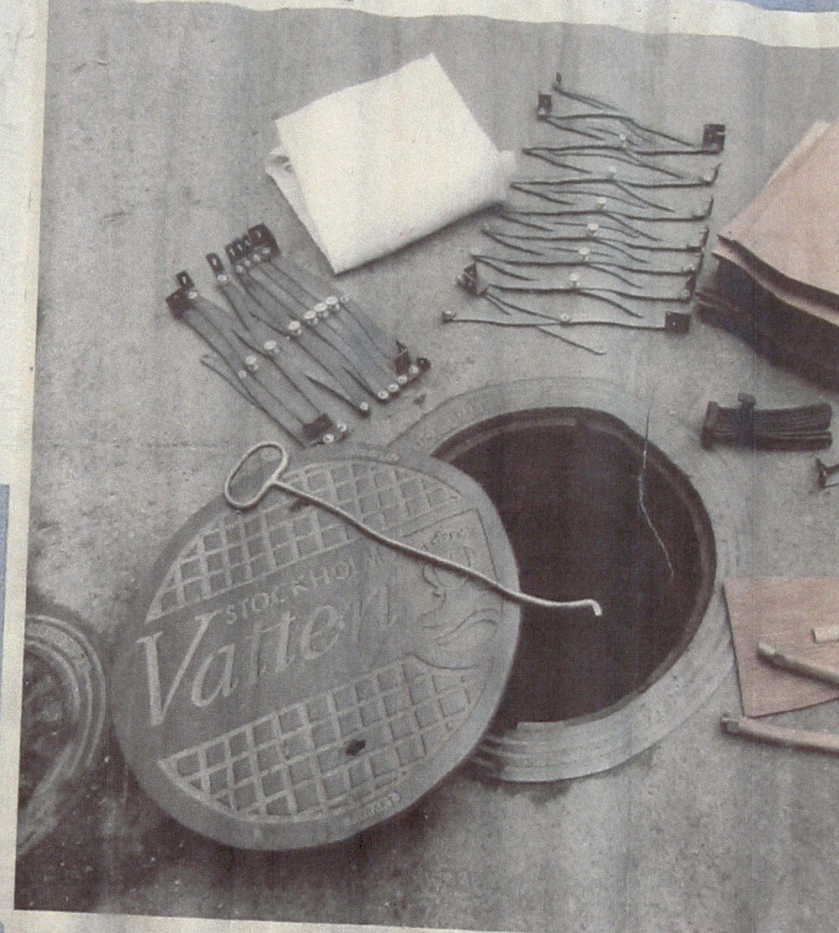

CROMBIE

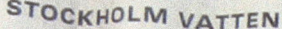

Vatten

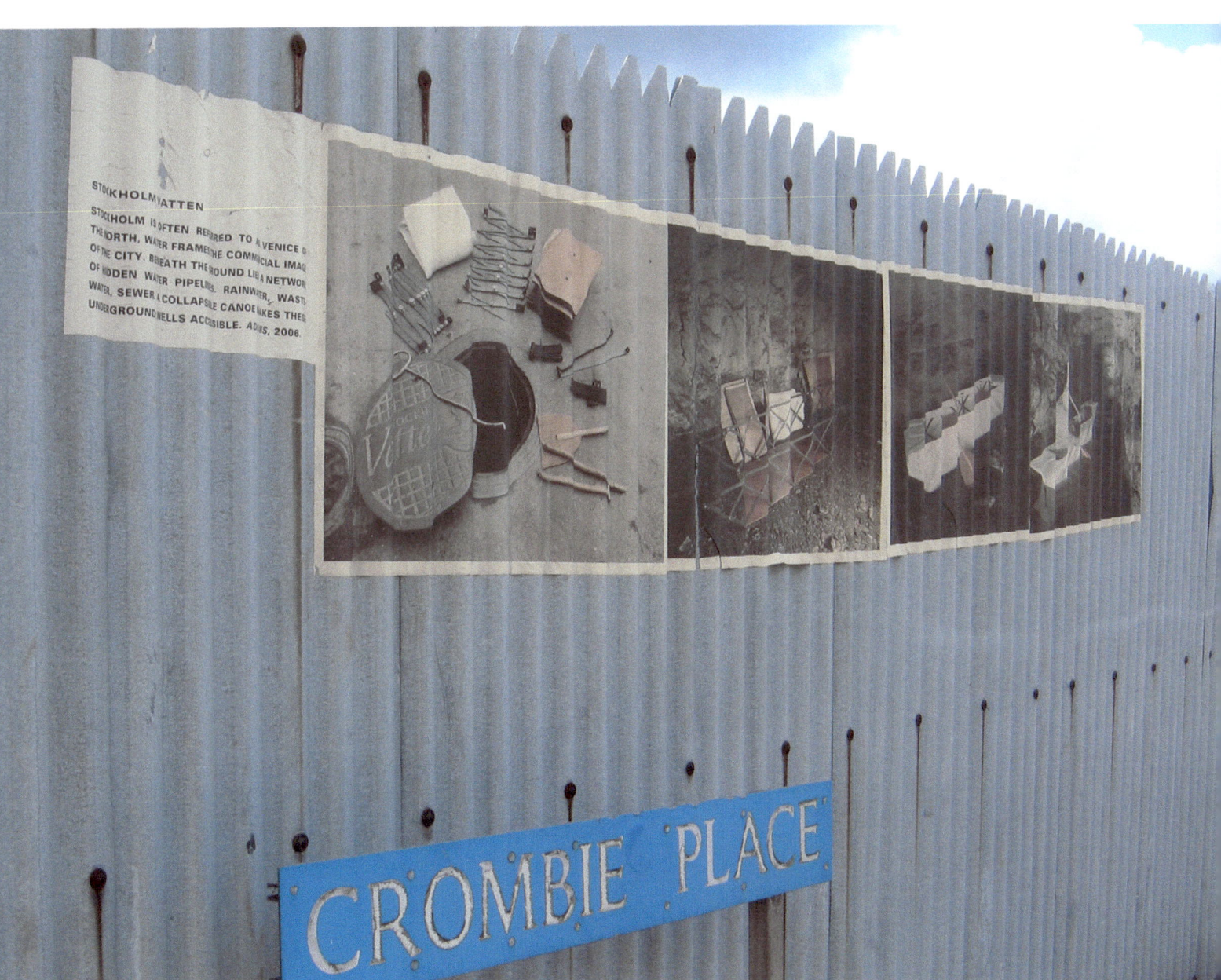

STOCKHOLMVATTEN

STOCKHOLM IS OFTEN REFERRED TO A VENICE O
THE NORTH, WATER FRAME THE COMMICIAL IMAG
OF THE CITY, BREATH THE ROUND LIE A NETWOR
OF HODEN WATER PIPELINS, RAINWATER, WAST
WATER, SEWER & COLLAPSLE CANOE LIKES THES
UNDERGROUND WELLS ACCISIBLE. ADIAS, 2006.

CROMBIE PLACE

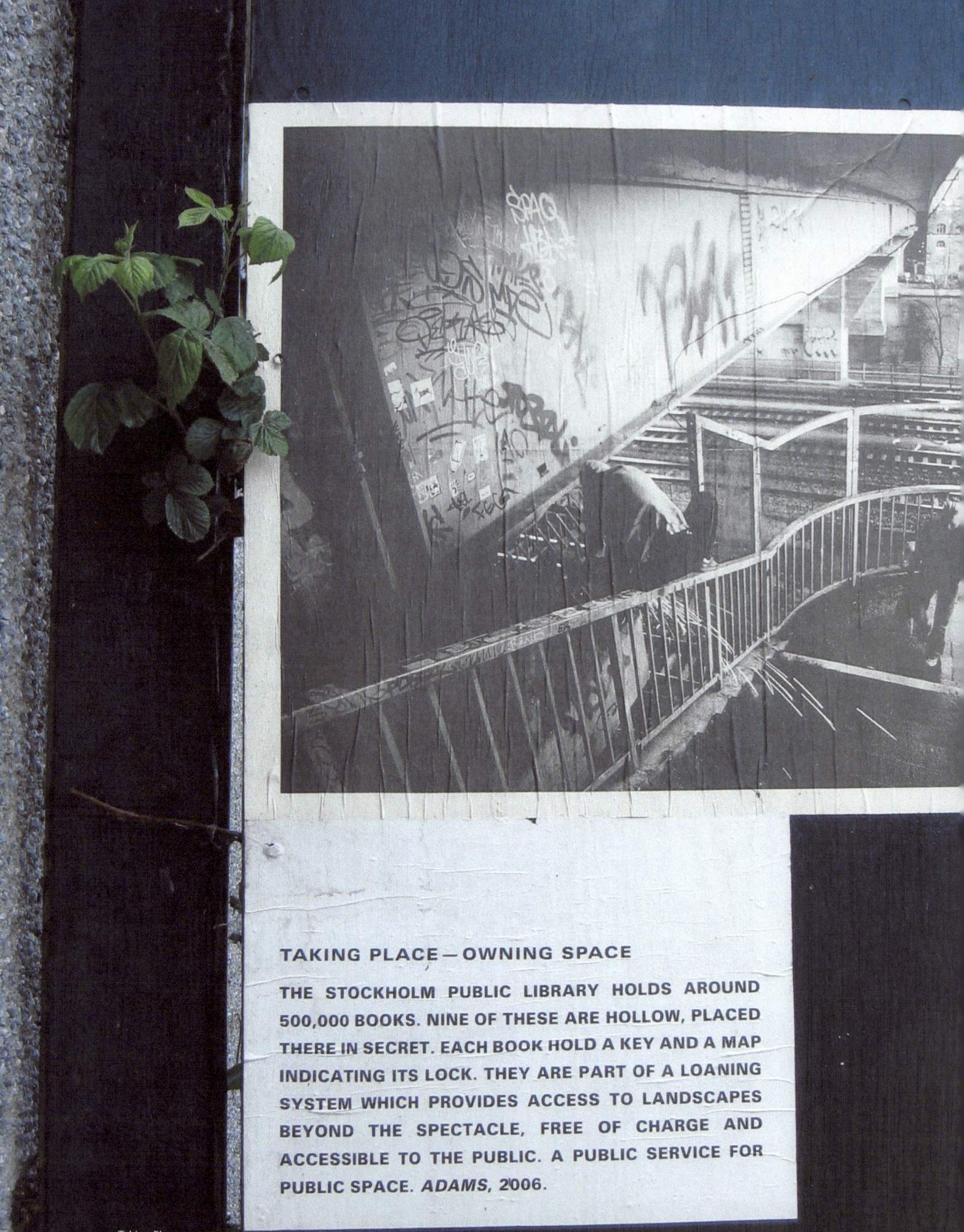

TAKING PLACE—OWNING SPACE

THE STOCKHOLM PUBLIC LIBRARY HOLDS AROUND 500,000 BOOKS. NINE OF THESE ARE HOLLOW, PLACED THERE IN SECRET. EACH BOOK HOLD A KEY AND A MAP INDICATING ITS LOCK. THEY ARE PART OF A LOANING SYSTEM WHICH PROVIDES ACCESS TO LANDSCAPES BEYOND THE SPECTACLE, FREE OF CHARGE AND ACCESSIBLE TO THE PUBLIC. A PUBLIC SERVICE FOR PUBLIC SPACE. *ADAMS, 2006.*

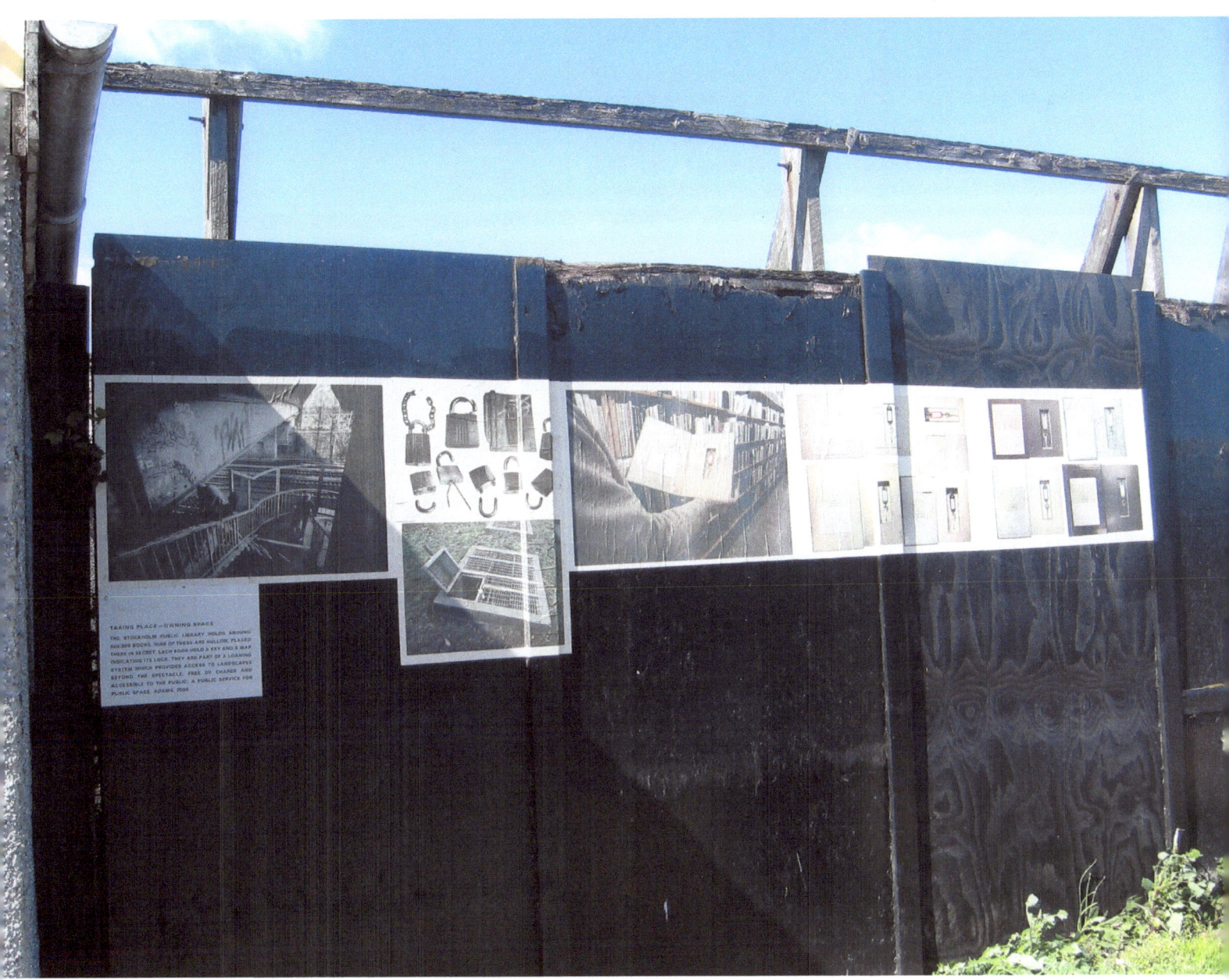

TAKING PLACE—OWNING SPACE

THE STOCKHOLM PUBLIC LIBRARY HOLDS AROUND
800,000 BOOKS. SOME OF THESE ARE HOLLOW, PLACED
THERE IN SECRET. EACH BOOK HOLD A KEY AND A MAP
INDICATING ITS LOCK. THEY ARE PART OF A LOANING
SYSTEM WHICH PROVIDES ACCESS TO LANDSCAPES
BEYOND THE SPECTACLE. FREE OF CHARGE AND
ACCESSIBLE TO THE PUBLIC: A PUBLIC SERVICE FOR
PUBLIC SPACE. ADAMS, 2006

AKAY, KIDPELE AND MADE

PRIVATE THOUGHTS FOR PUBLIC PLACES is an ongoing project
— which means we're working on it. The idea is that secrets are
left behind like whispers, echoes or scars in the places where
people have been. If a feeling is big enough, it leaves a mark.
Guilt and regret leave smudges everywhere. Stains. It's rare to
find a fossil of a happy memory. Happy memories fade. But all
the darkest secrets leave shadows in the city.

Or maybe we just made all that up.

Maybe MADE and AKAY just go out and look for the odd and
unnoticed parts of the city, find a way to unscrew them and
stuff them in their backpacks. They tell KIDPELE where they
got it, affectionately known as 'the spot'. She mumbles what
she thinks the funniest or most heartbreaking thing would be to
write. They go to their toolbox and take out their toys and etch,
pound and engrave texts into the pieces. Then they put it back
where it came from and wait for someone to recognize the scab
of a secret.

[APA]

SECRETS

FOR

SECRET

SPACES

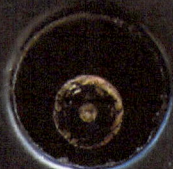

I TOLD
YOU I
WOULDN'T
SHOW THE
TAPE TO
ANYONE,
BUT I
PLAYED IT
FOR YOUR
FRIENDS.
THEY ALL
DIED
LAUGHING.

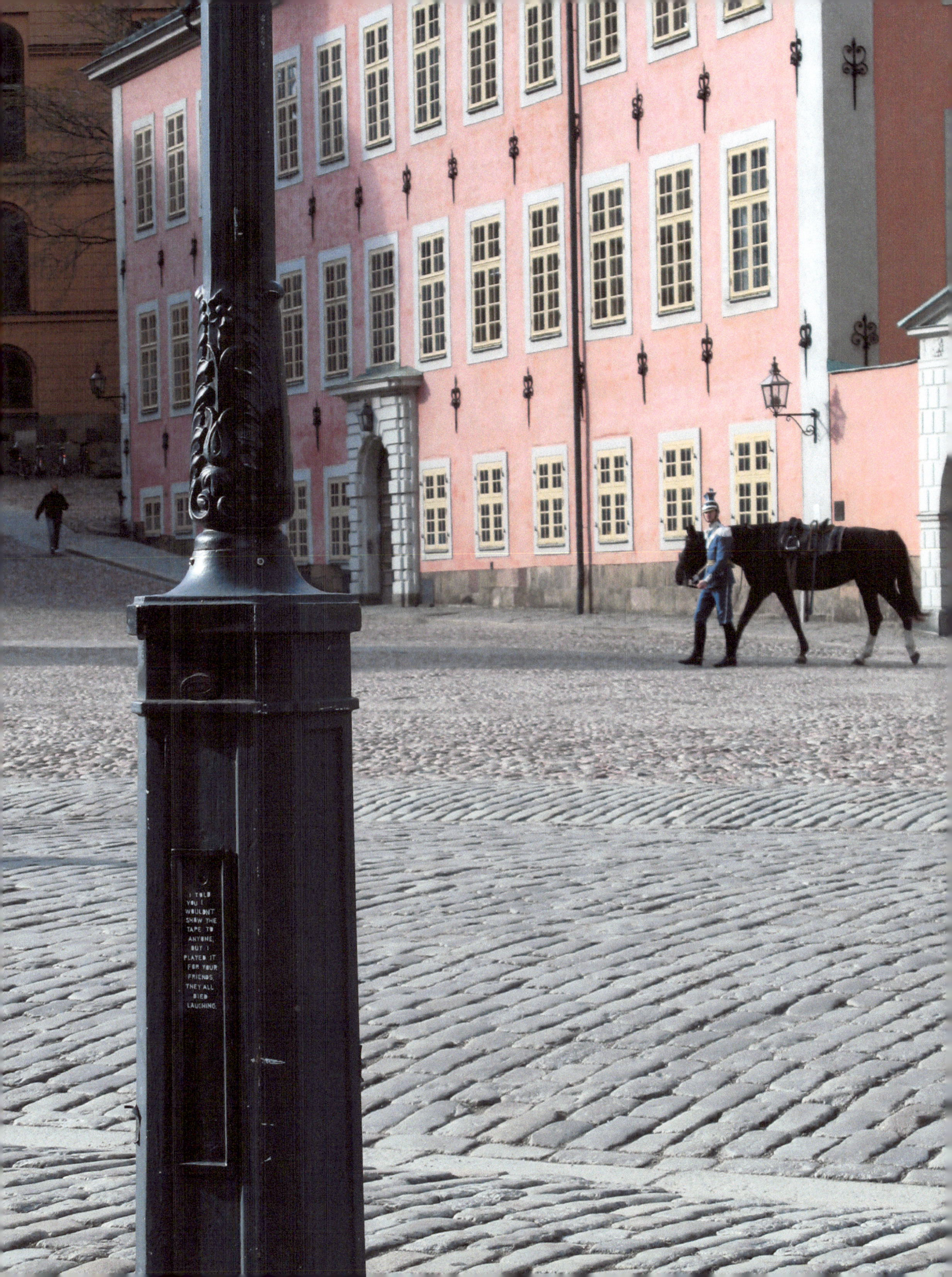

I TOLD
YOU I
WOULDN'T
SHOW THE
TAPE TO
ANYONE,
BUT I
PLAYED IT
FOR YOUR
FRIENDS.
THEY ALL
DIED
LAUGHING.

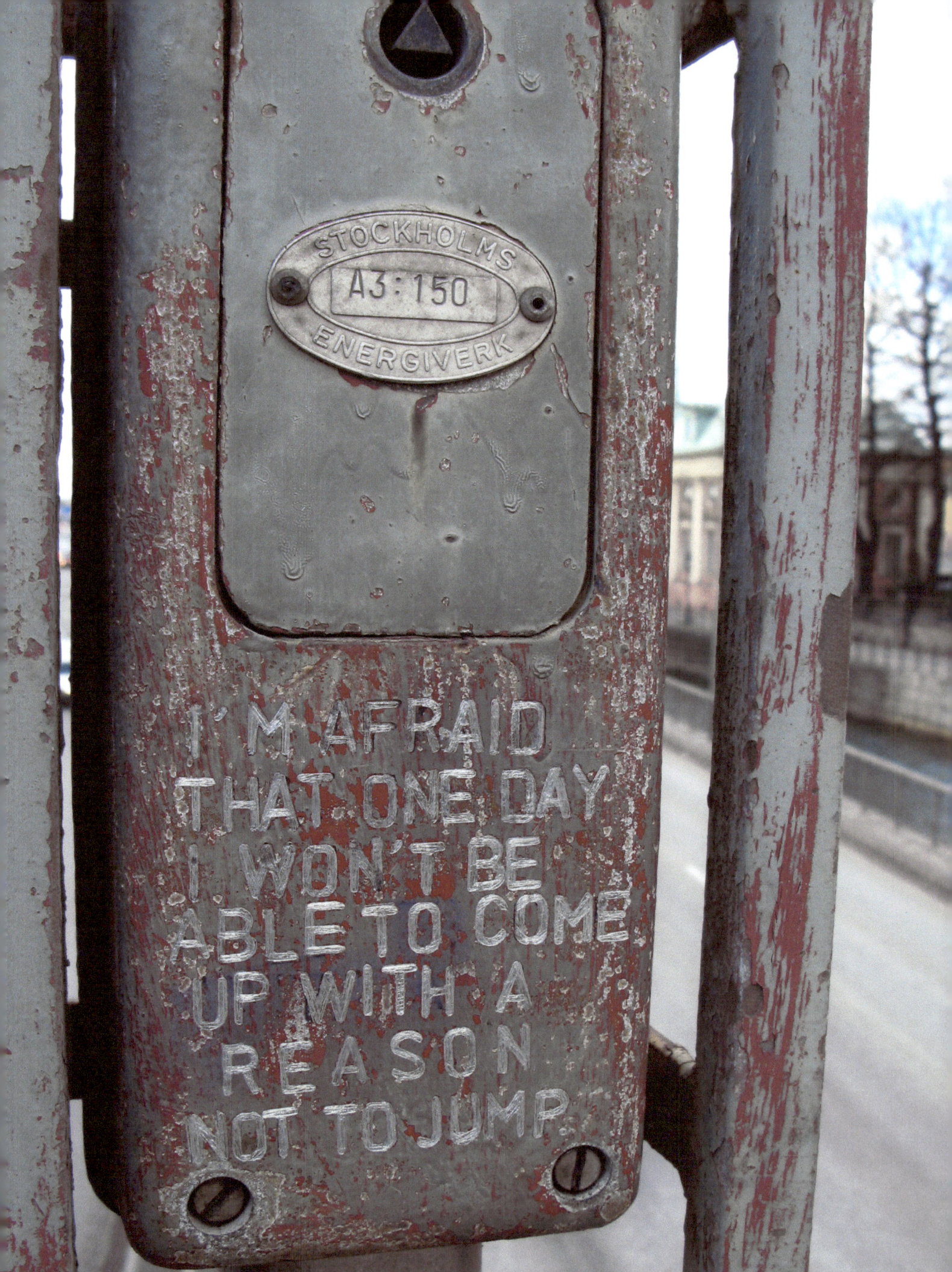

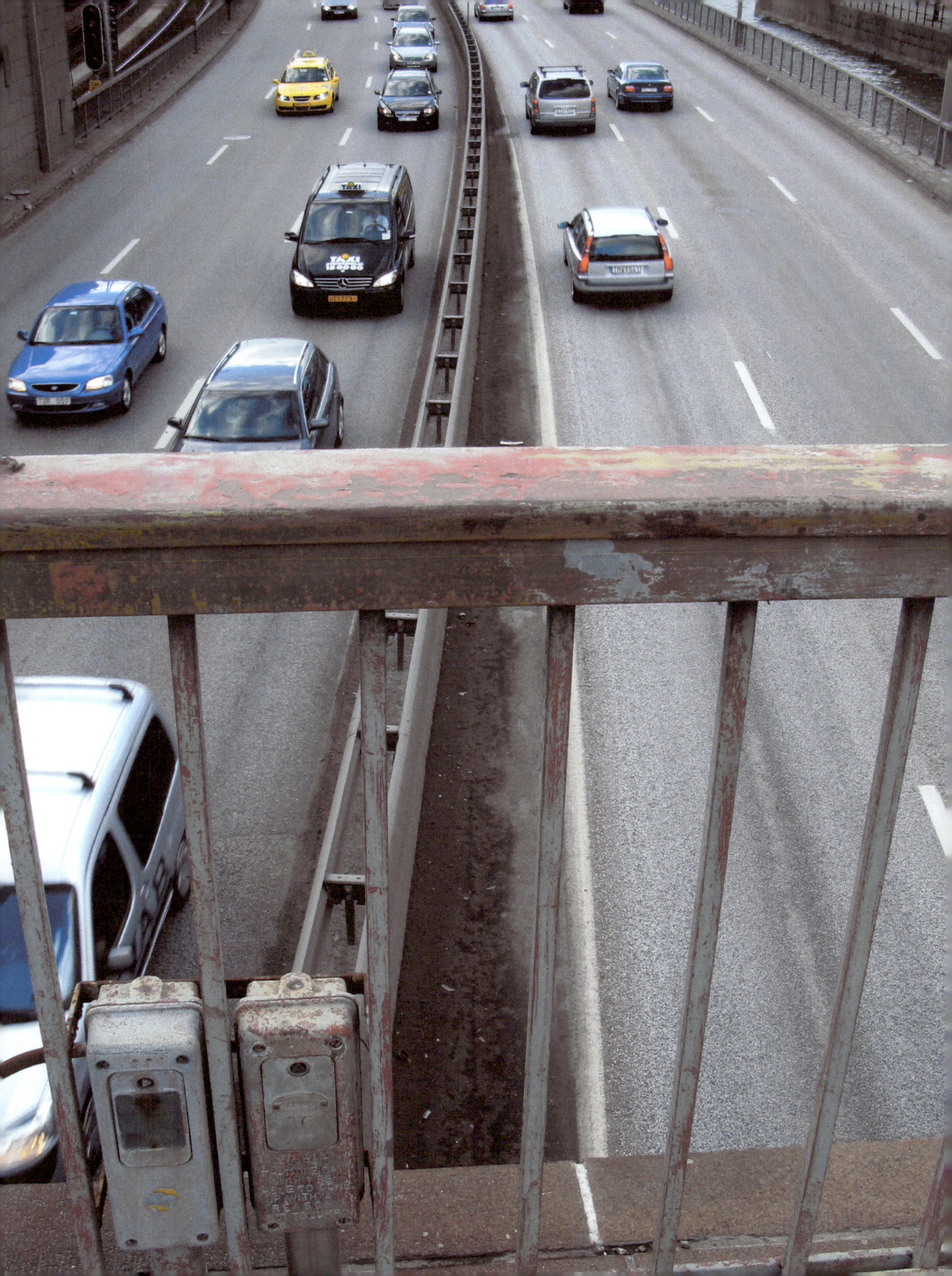

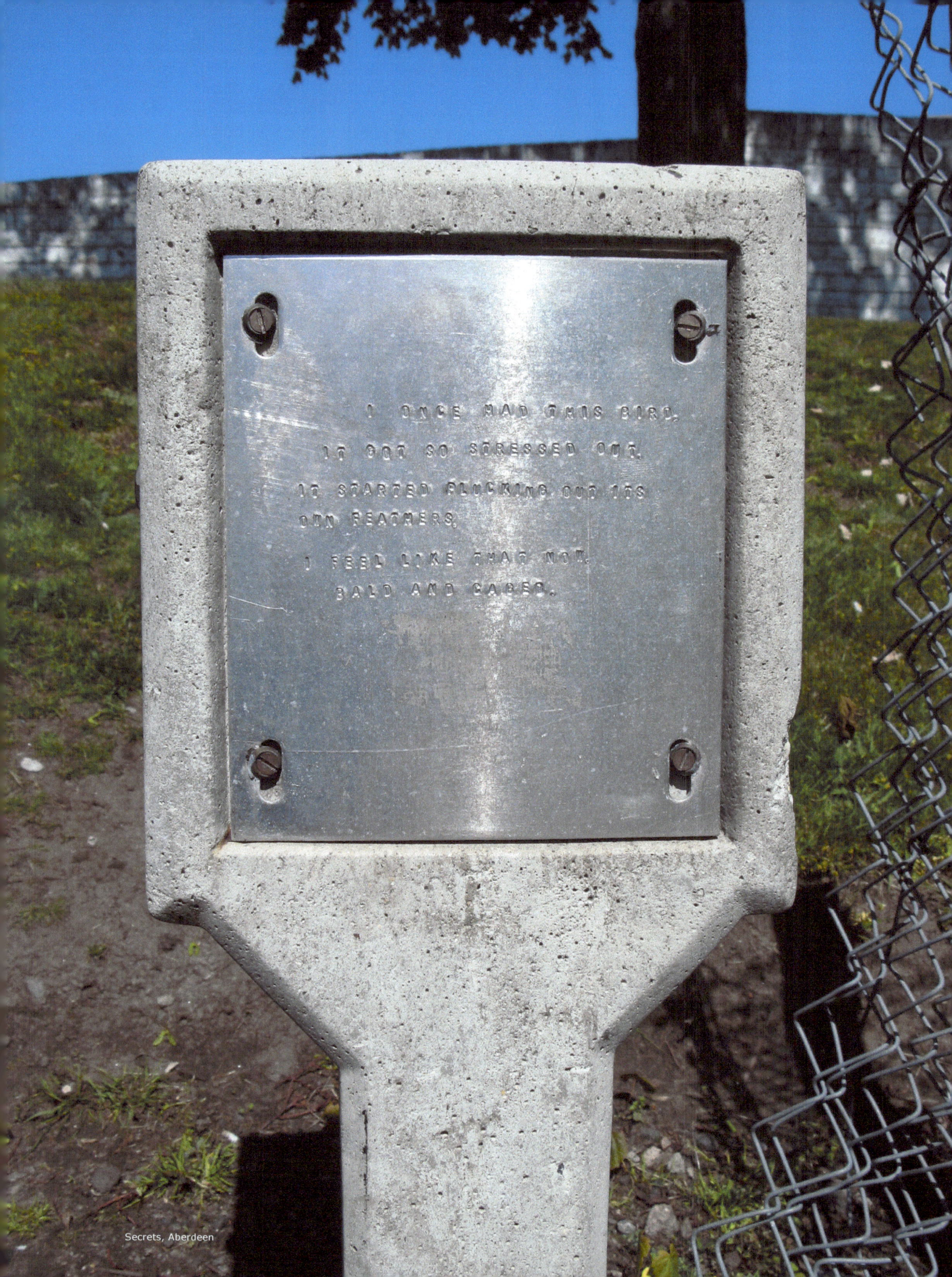

I ONCE HAD THIS BIRD.
IT GOT SO STRESSED OUT,
IT STARTED PLUCKING OUT ITS
OWN FEATHERS.
I FEEL LIKE THAT NOW,
BALD AND CAGED.

Secrets, Aberdeen

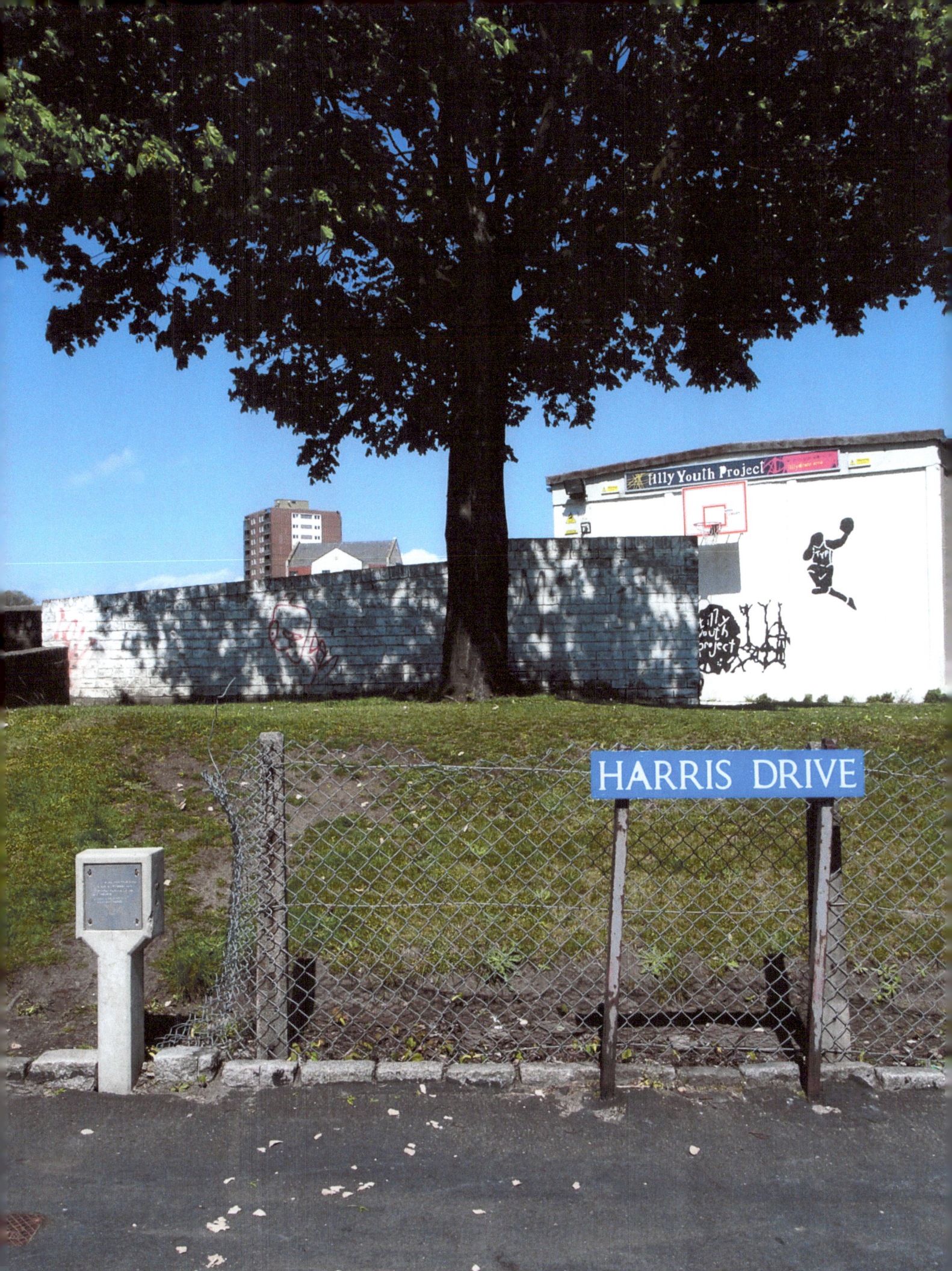

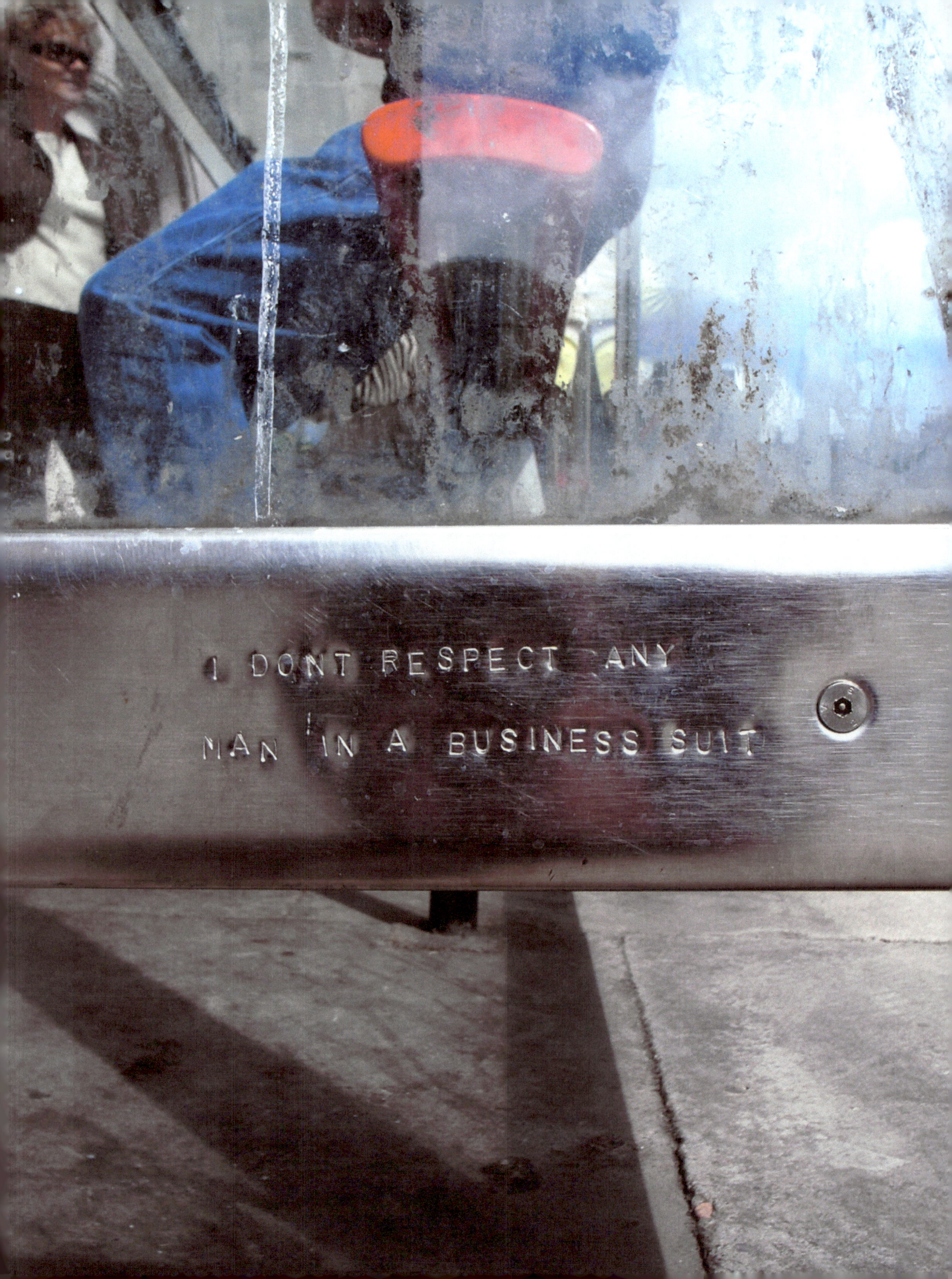

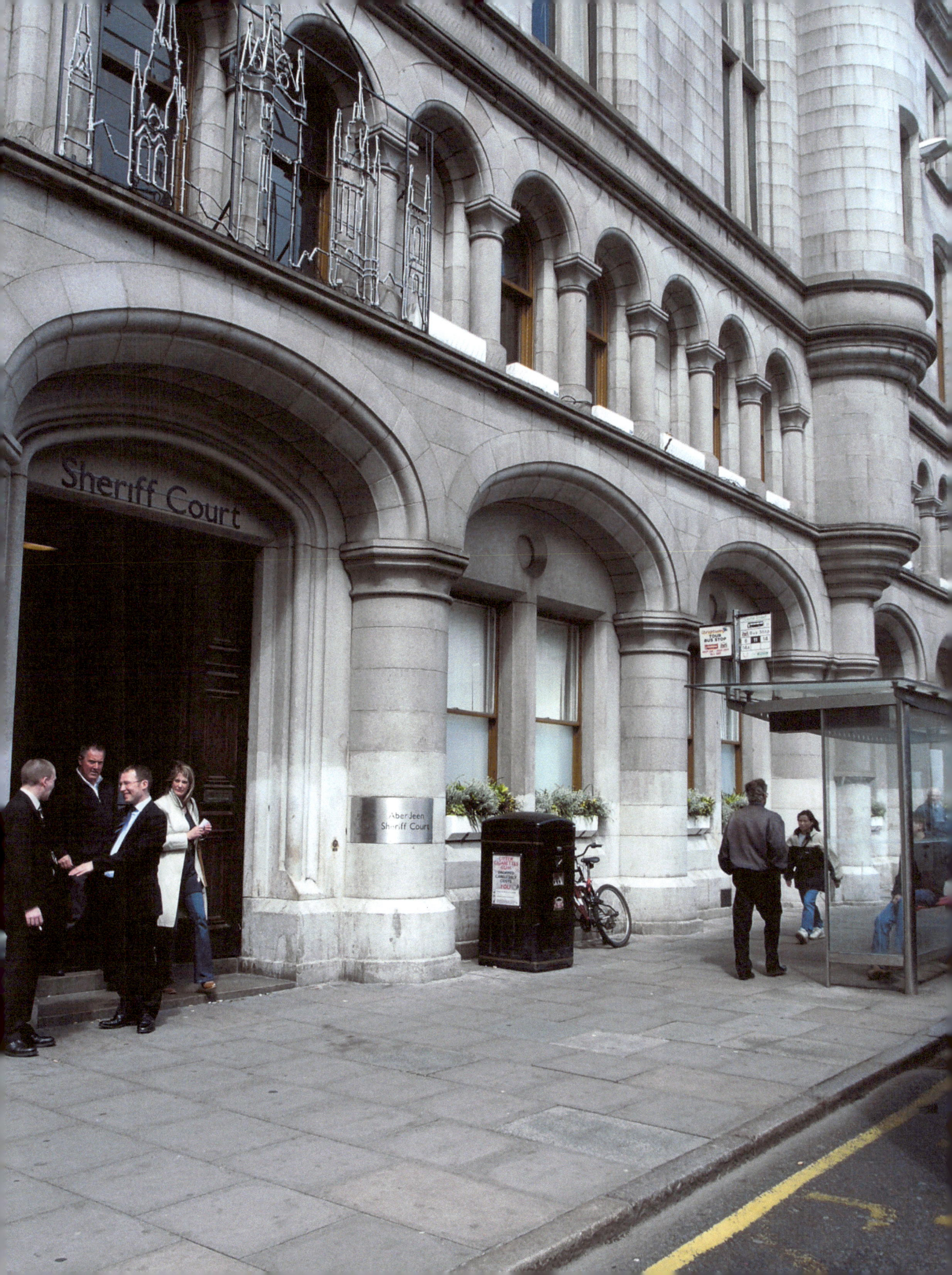

PUSH

I LOVE

ROMANTIC

COMEDIES

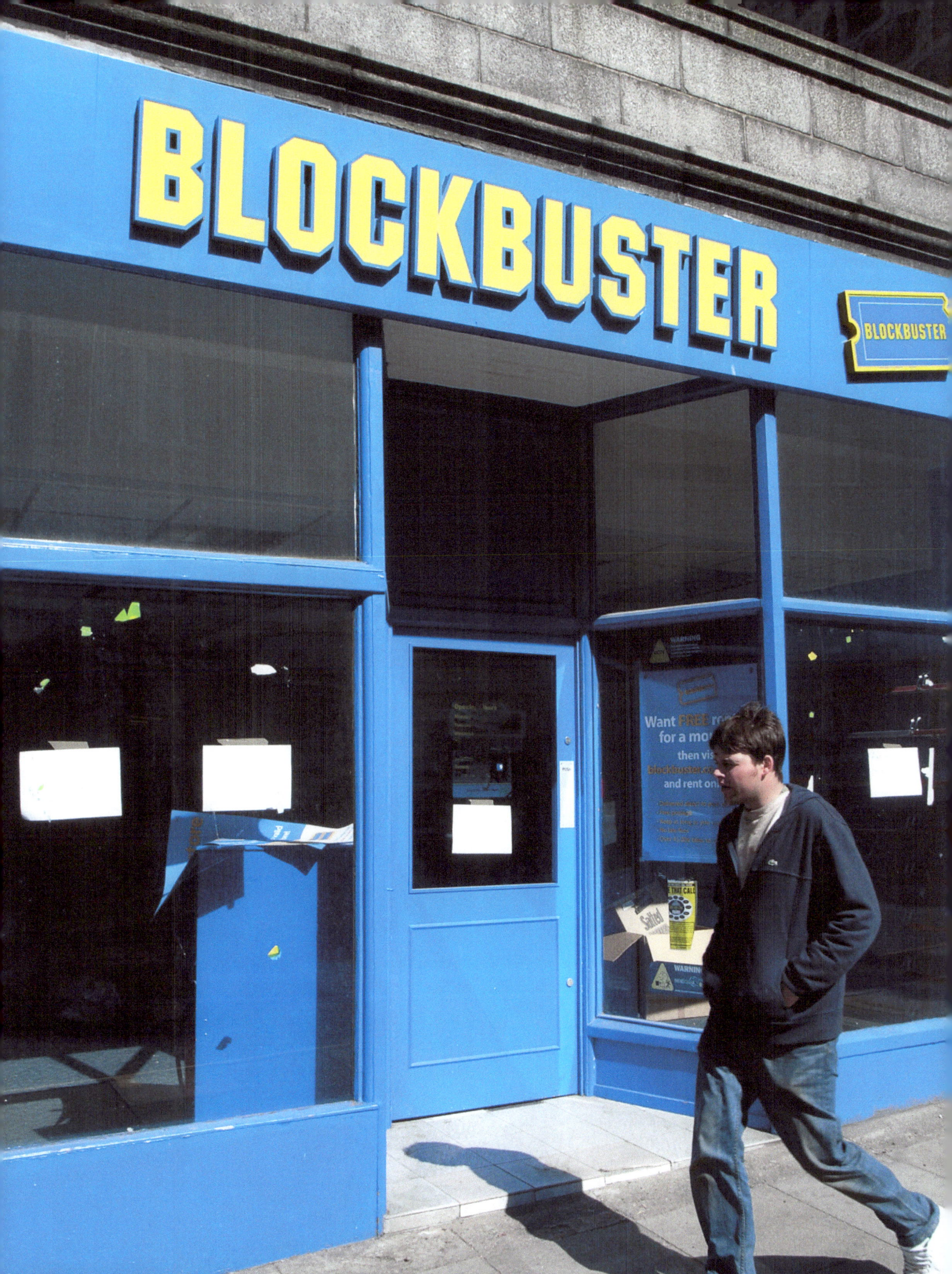

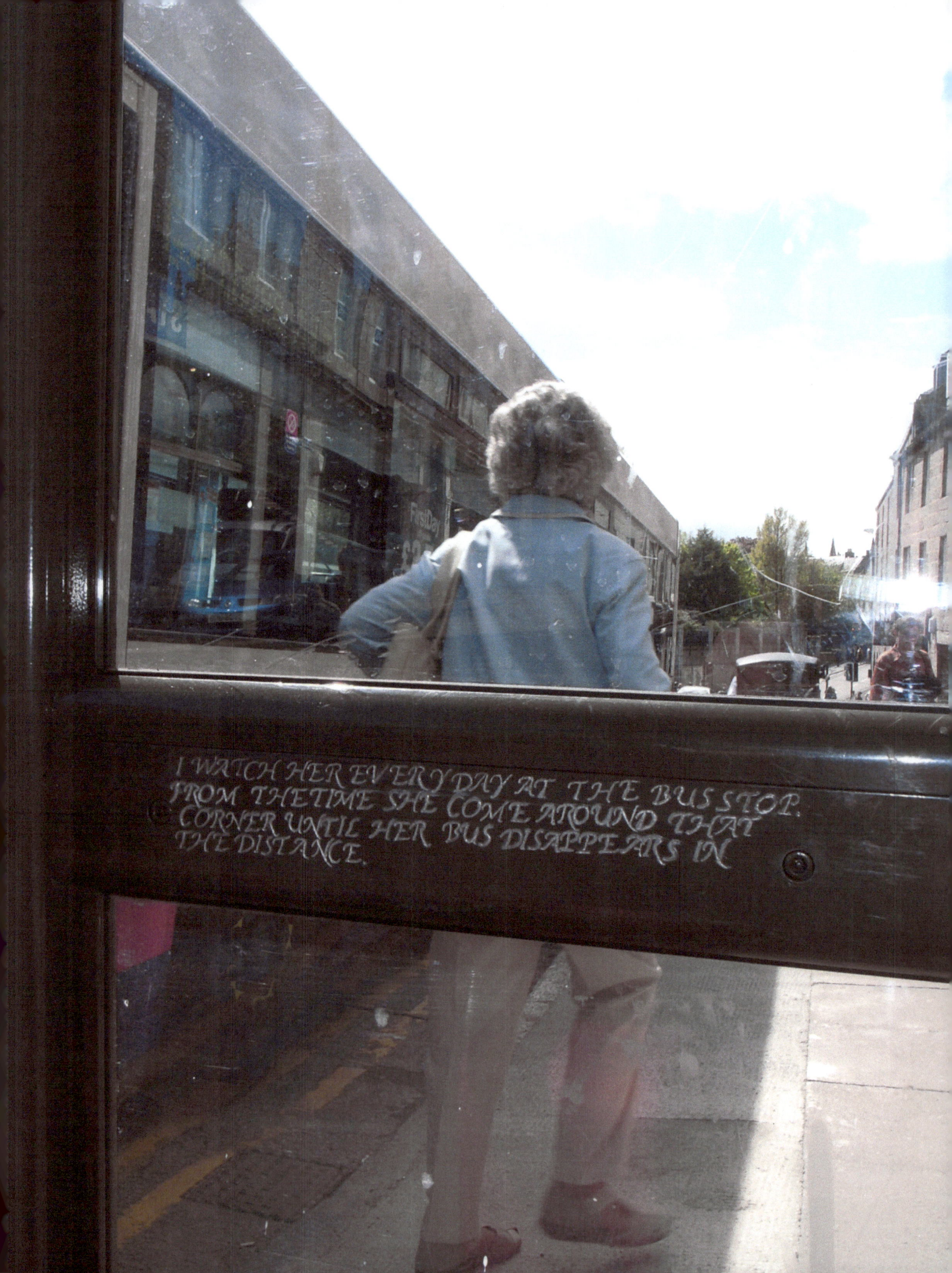

I WATCH HER EVERY DAY AT THE BUS STOP. FROM THE TIME SHE COME AROUND THAT CORNER UNTIL HER BUS DISAPPEARS IN THE DISTANCE.

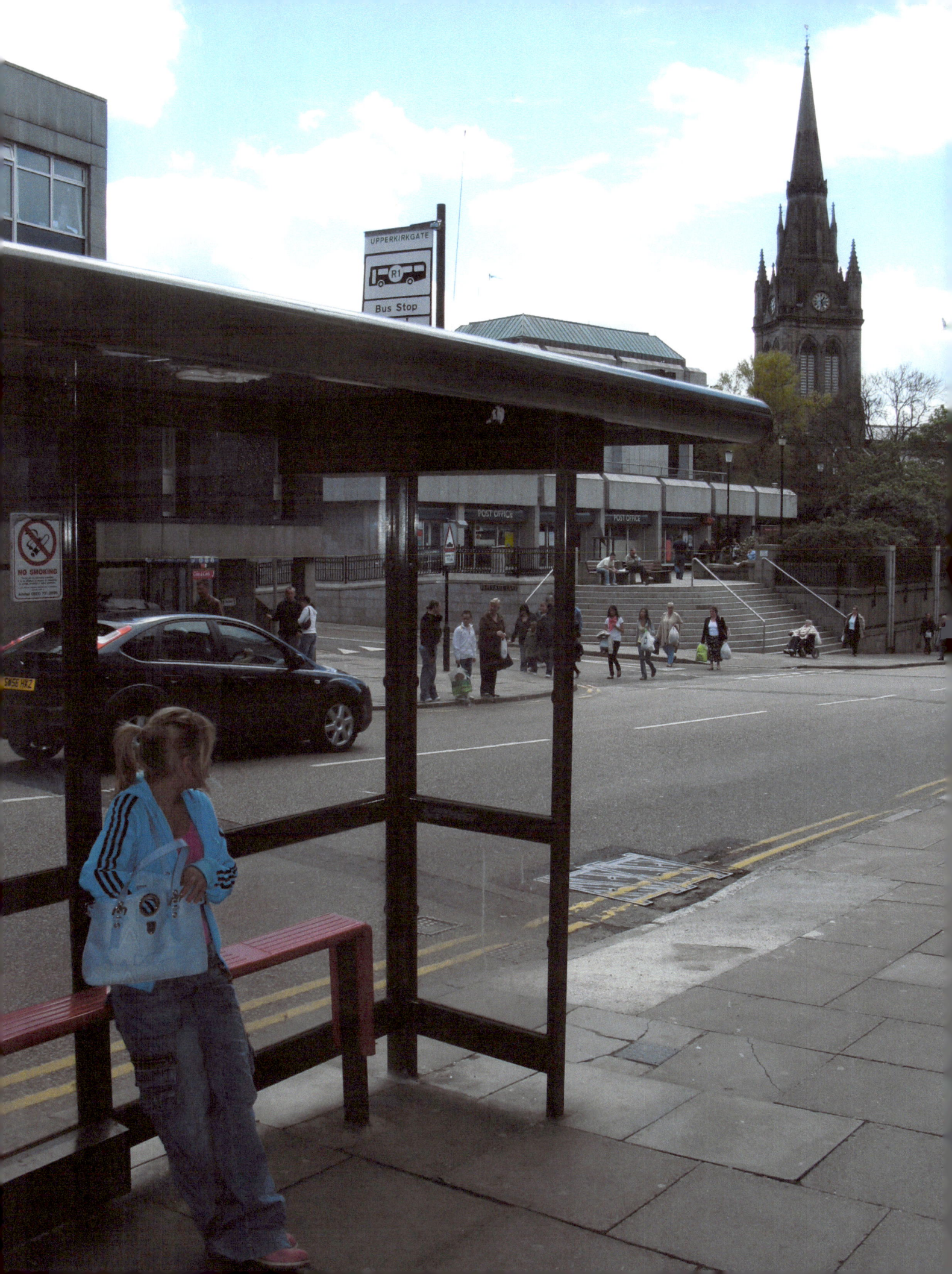

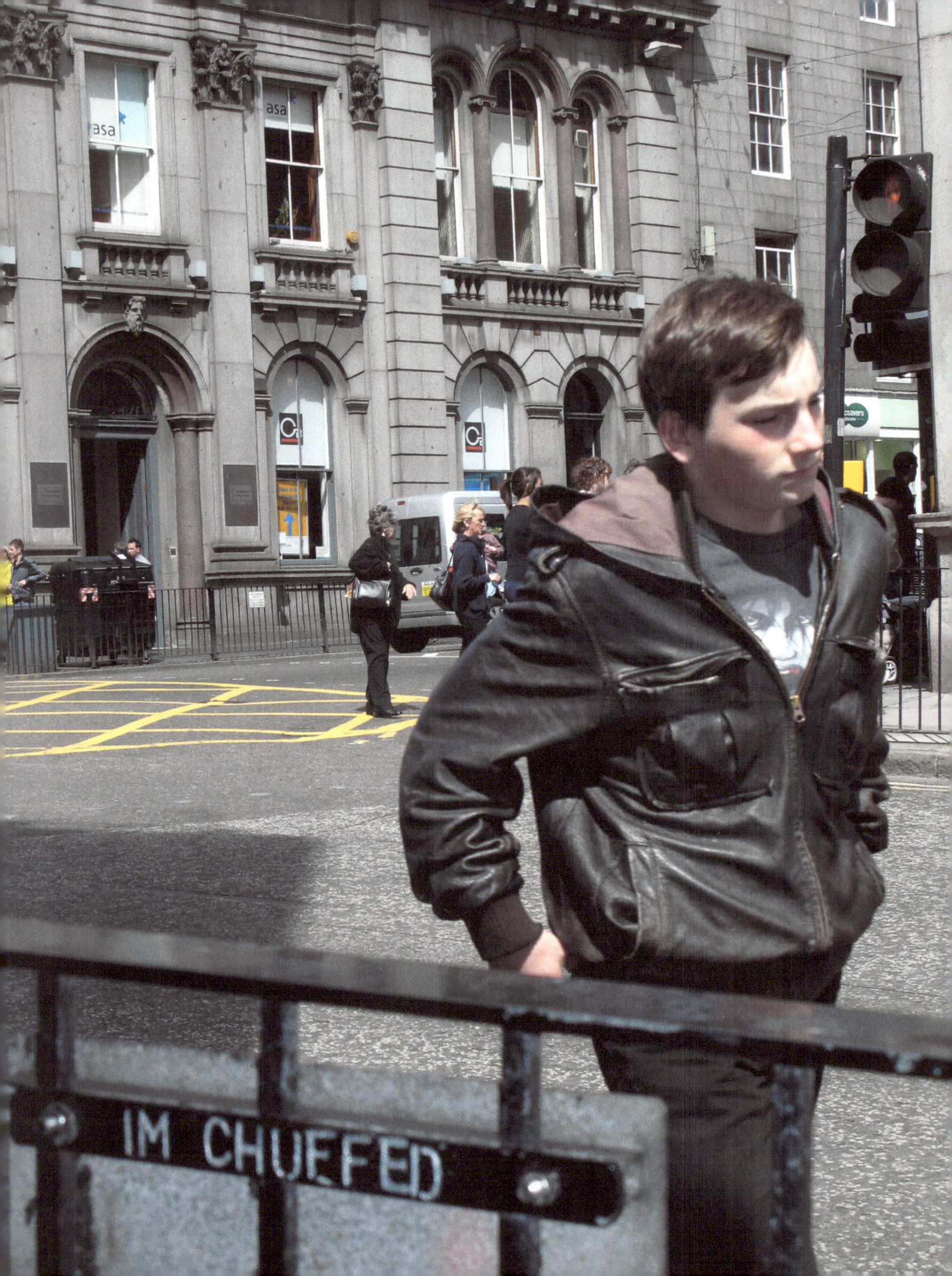

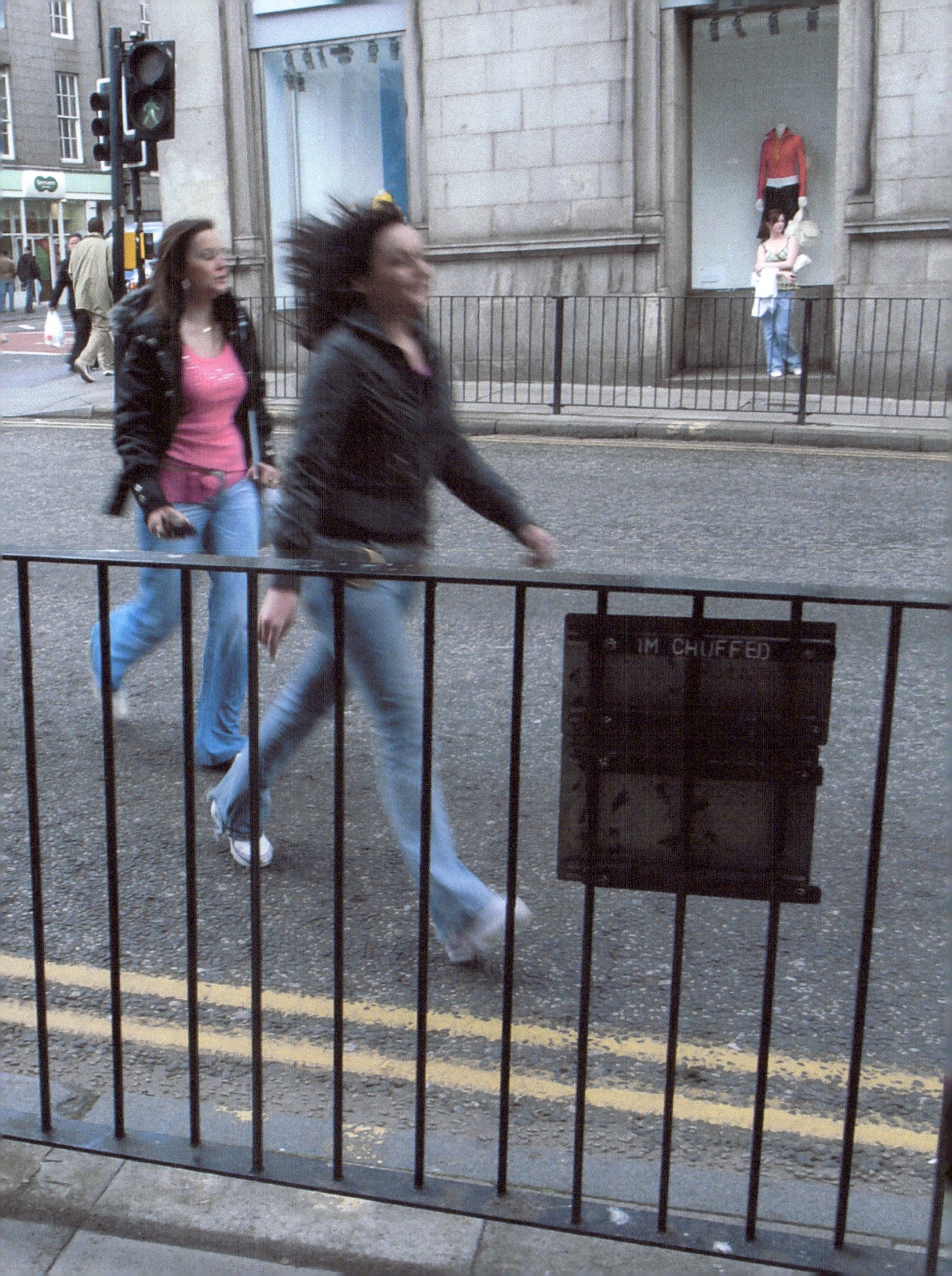

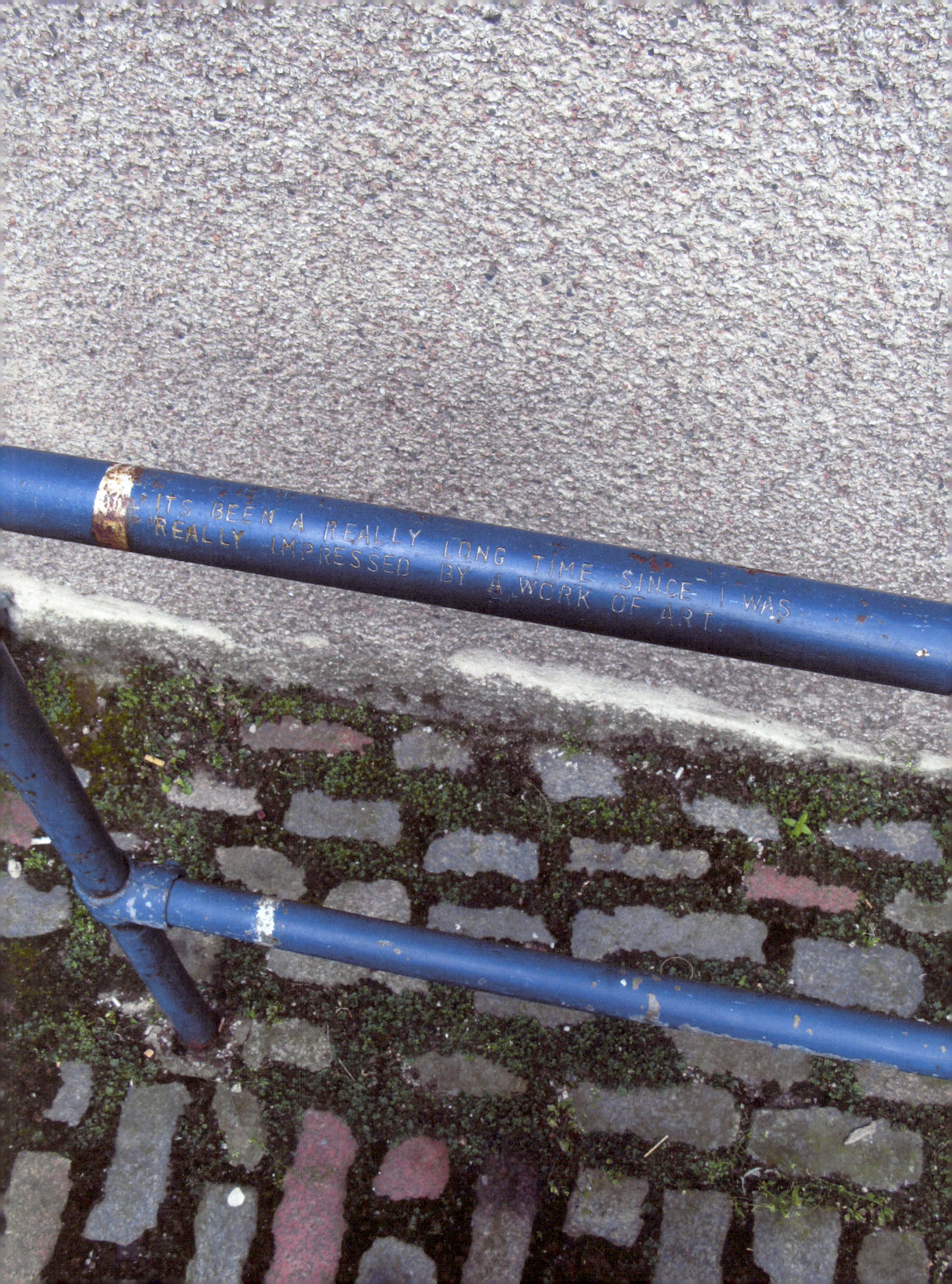

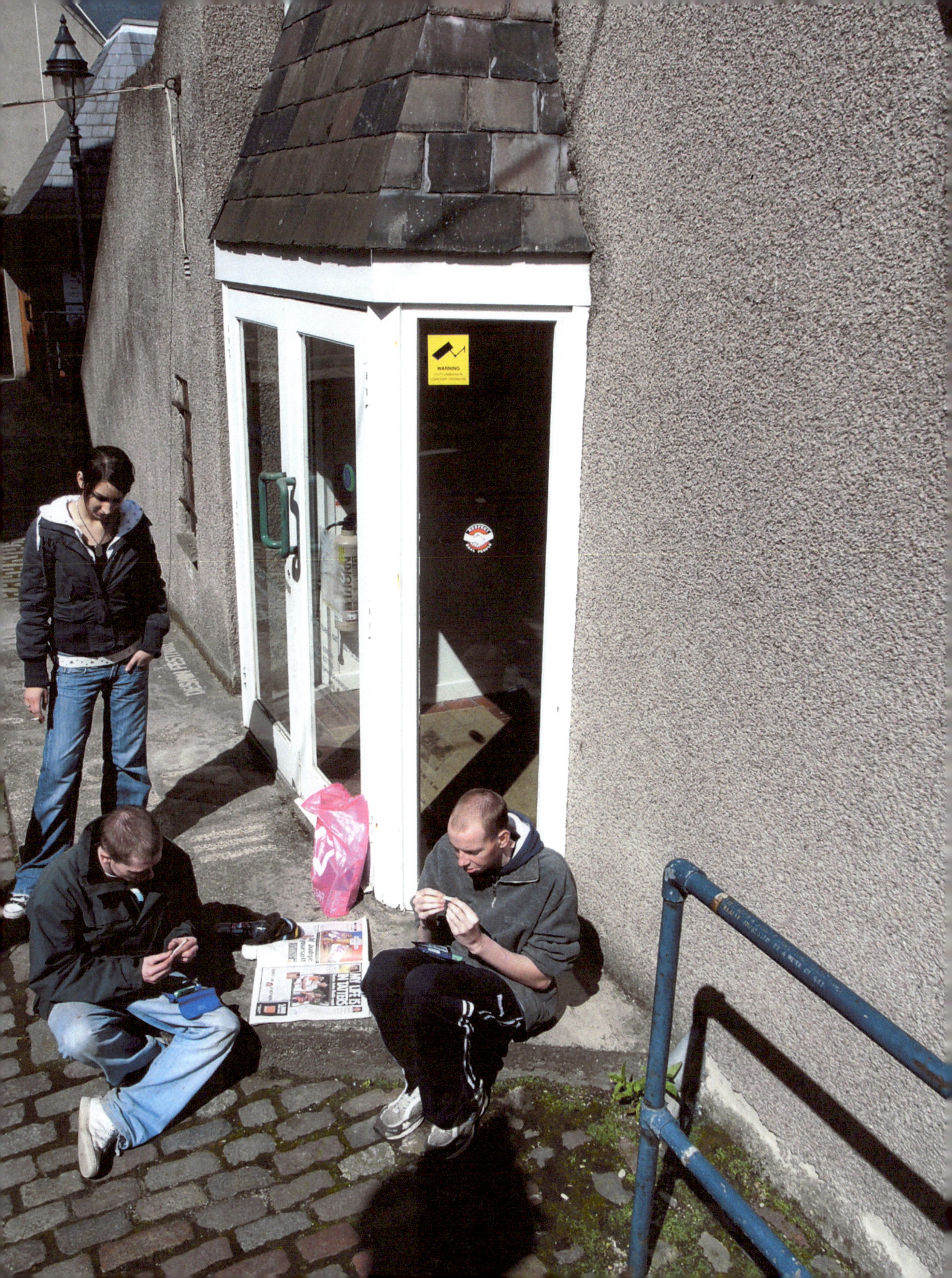

BRETT BLOOM AND BONNIE FORTUNE

In 1965, president of the United States, Lyndon B. Johnson was presented with a report on a new problem: climate change. This report, prepared by top scientists of the day, did not include plans for the reduction of carbon emissions, the biggest contributor to this problem, it suggested instead a plan to "spread 'very small reflecting particles' across the ocean surface to reflect light and heat back into space."[1] This interesting idea spawned a host of geo-engineering concepts from building giant reflectors for the sun's rays to blasting seawater into the air to create a cooling effect, all to turn back the tide of climate change.

'Cradle to Cradle: Remaking the way we make things' by William McDonough and Michael Braungart offers histories of production and practical steps for rethinking the way we produce material goods and services. They suggest that as we have evolved so should our production practices and the capitalist model can co-exist with the environment through design that acknowledges the intelligence of natural systems. Their book calls for a new sustainable paradigm brought about through human engineering.

Our project 'Refuse, Refuse' doesn't sit all that comfortably with these ideas and others that insist that the mechanisms that created global warming and other ecological disasters are the ones to solve them. We think that our engineering practices have brought us to our current environmental and cultural situation and that there is no better way to deal with the constant stream of waste running out of our factories than to stop, to refuse refuse. We are both attracted to and repelled by the idea of creating a solution out of the problem. Being able to create a new home out of recycled materials, or to inject the atmosphere with tiny reflectors to redirect heat away from the planet are both beautiful and Sisyphean.

In this book, you will find experiments with trash in Chicago and Aberdeen. These experiments are not solutions; they are a way for us to play, to engage, and to find some way around our frustration under the great weight of global capital. Our frustration leads us to wander the alleys of Chicago aimlessly finding garbage to make into flowers, simulacra of the natural world that represents the evolution to us of life under capital. With 100% of the world's oceans contaminated with some particles of plastic, the inevitable is that what once was the natural world is now engineered. Making art and making lamps are both "useful" even if we say they are not. They function within this art discourse as objects of contemplation. As artists, we do not want to distract from the fact that solving the problems will take everyone working on them together. The most complicated design or theory is no replacement for thinking and doing things completely differently than we have.

[Brett Bloom and Bonnie Fortune]

[1] "Plan B for global warming?", The Economist, March 8th, 2007

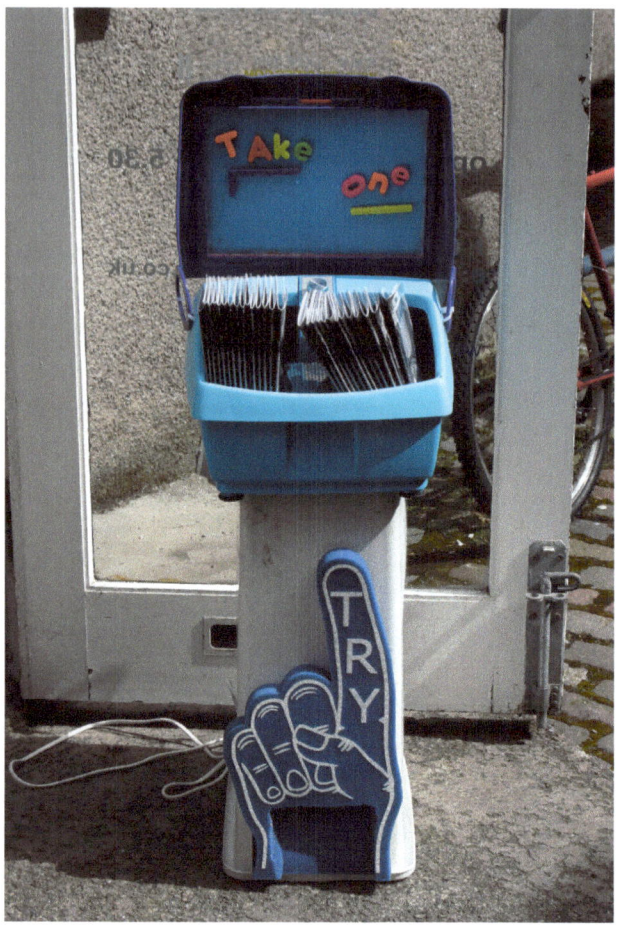

Refuse Refuse
Offset cover that folds out into an A3-sized poster, 20 offset pages

This booklet continues several inquiries and activities as we add another book to the library, make bouquets large and small out of found trash, continue our research into interesting projects involving the urban nights sky, and have several how-to pages. Download from http://www.letsremake.info/publications.html
ISBN 978-0-9555524-1-0

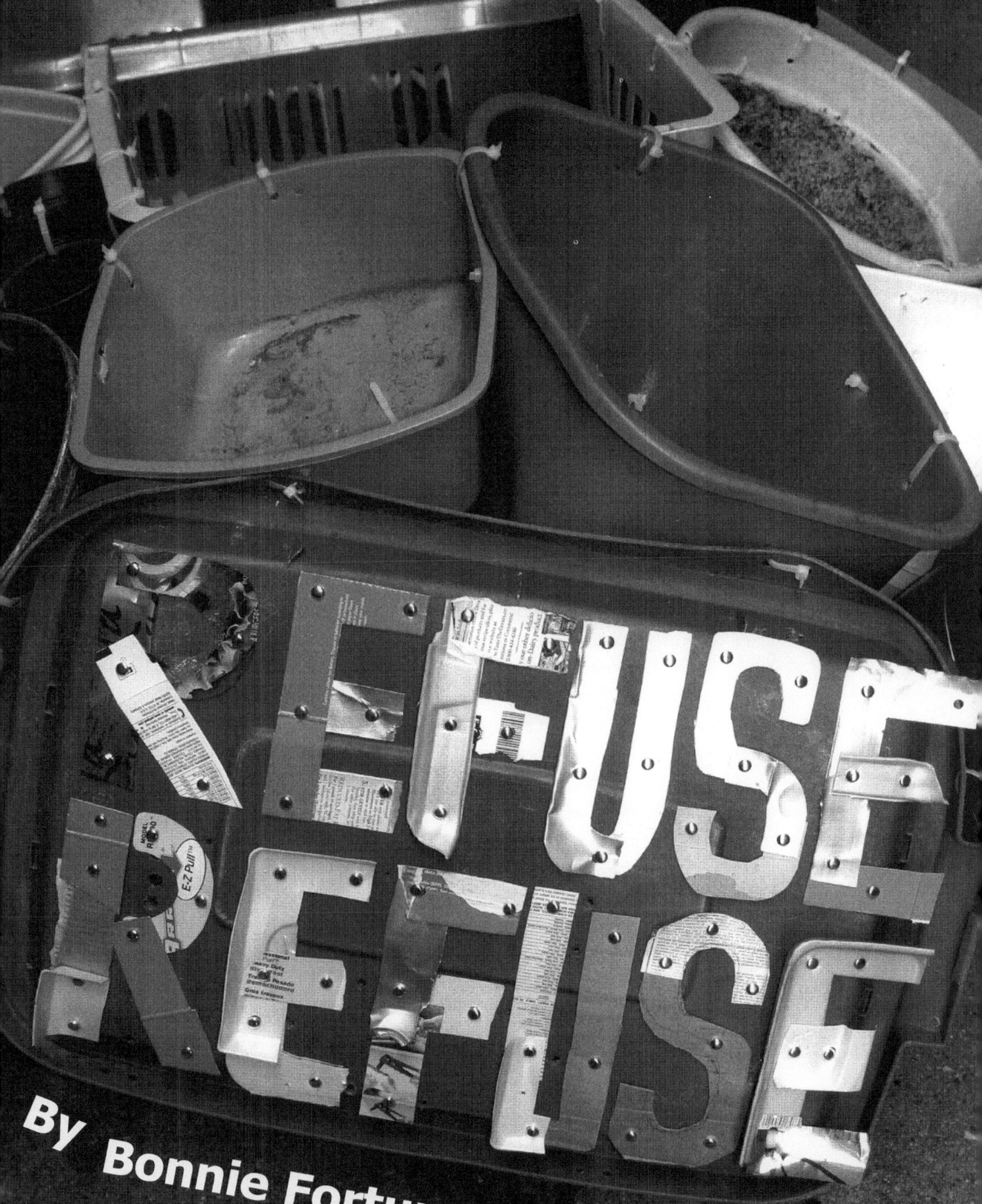

REFUSE
REFUSE

By Bonnie Fortune and Brett Bloom

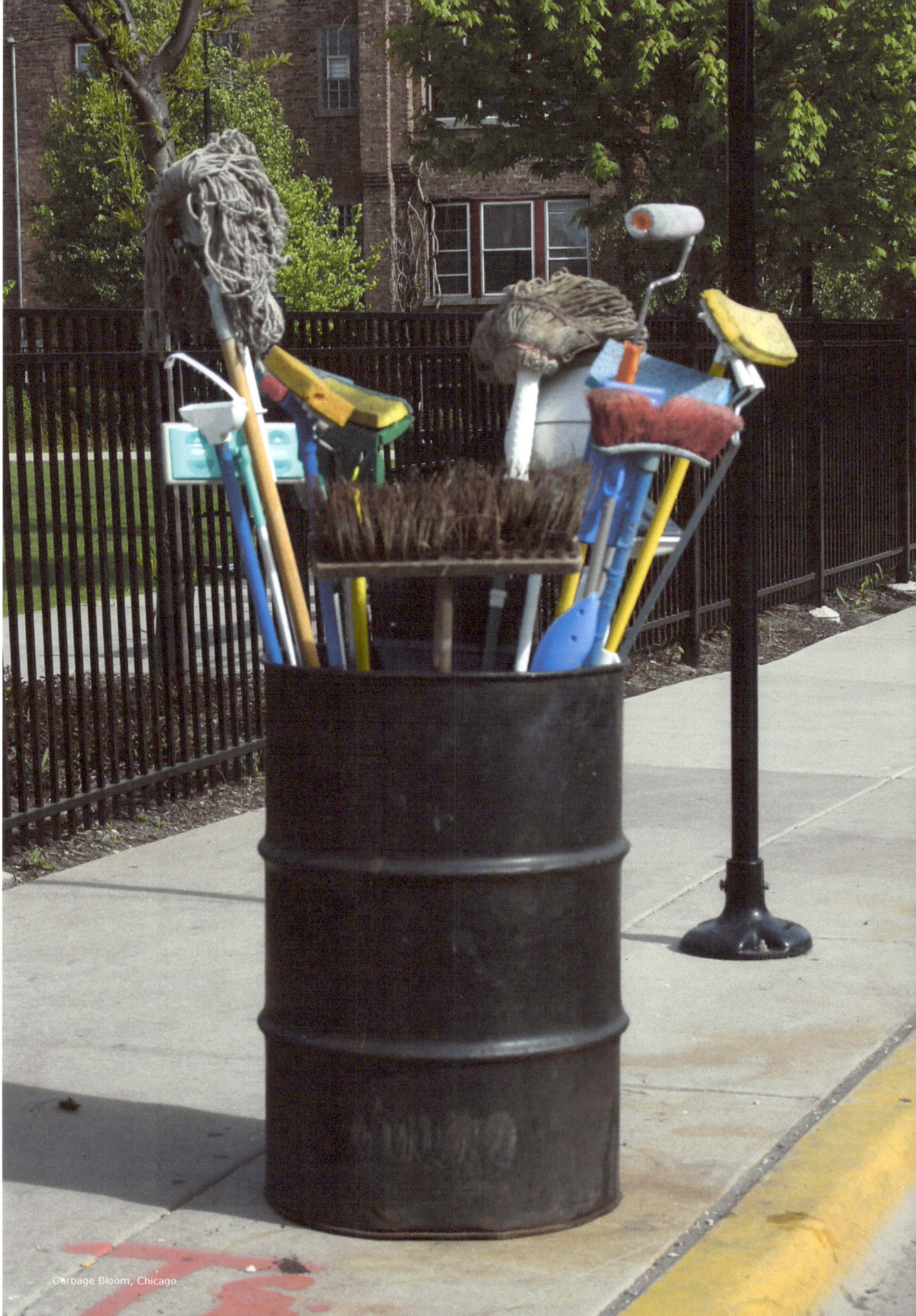

Garbage Bloom, Chicago

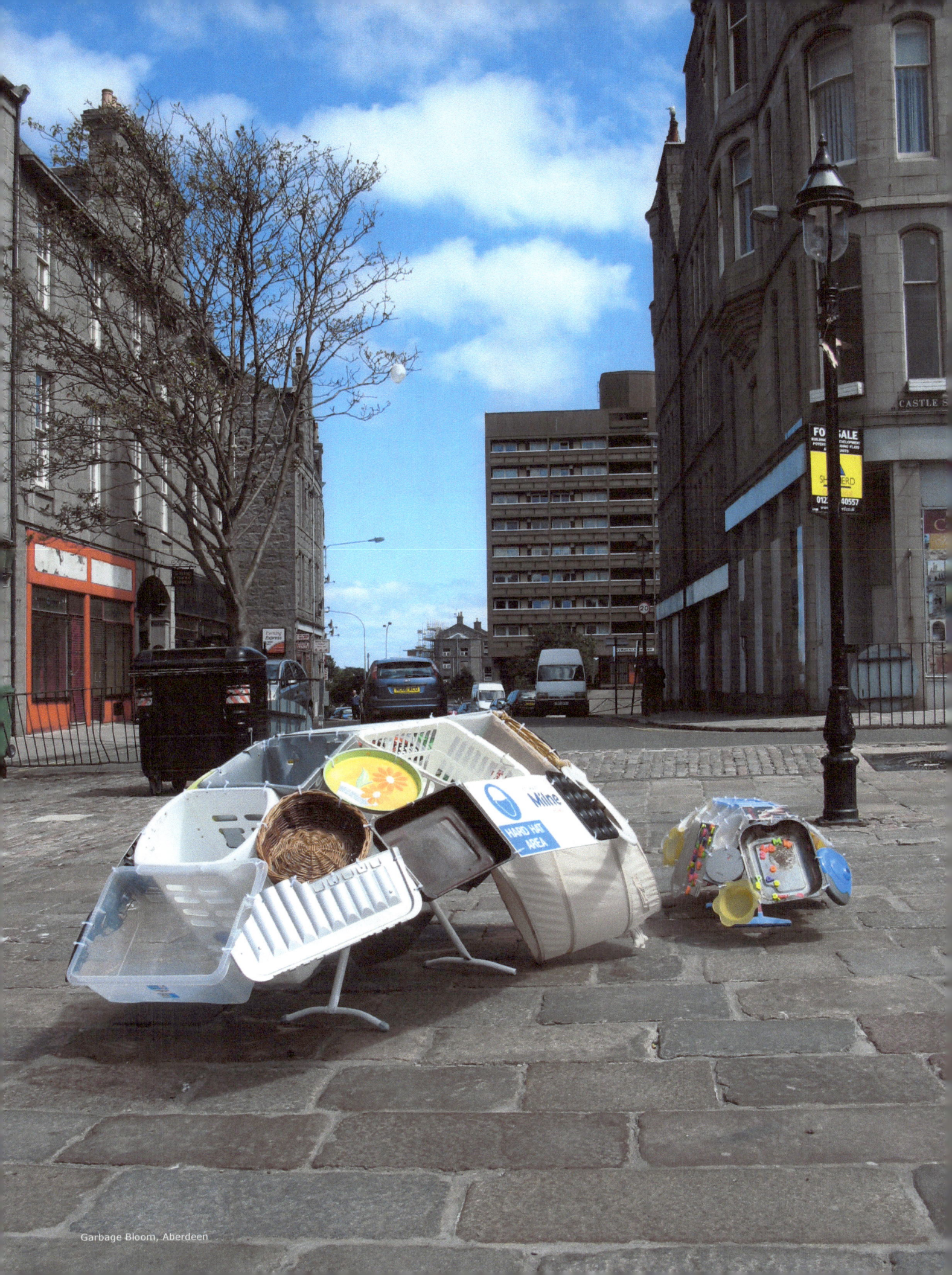

Garbage Bloom, Aberdeen

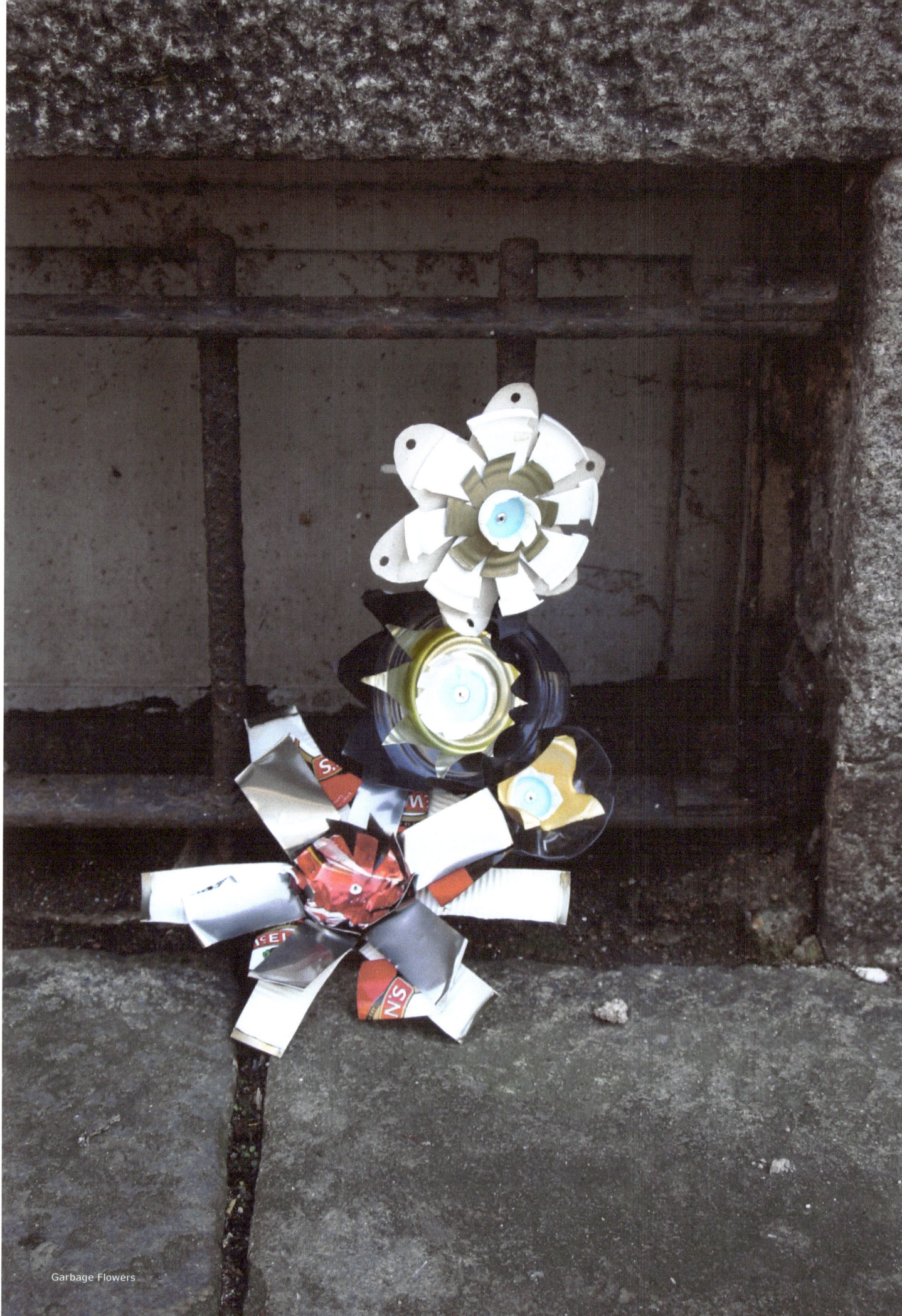

Garbage Flowers

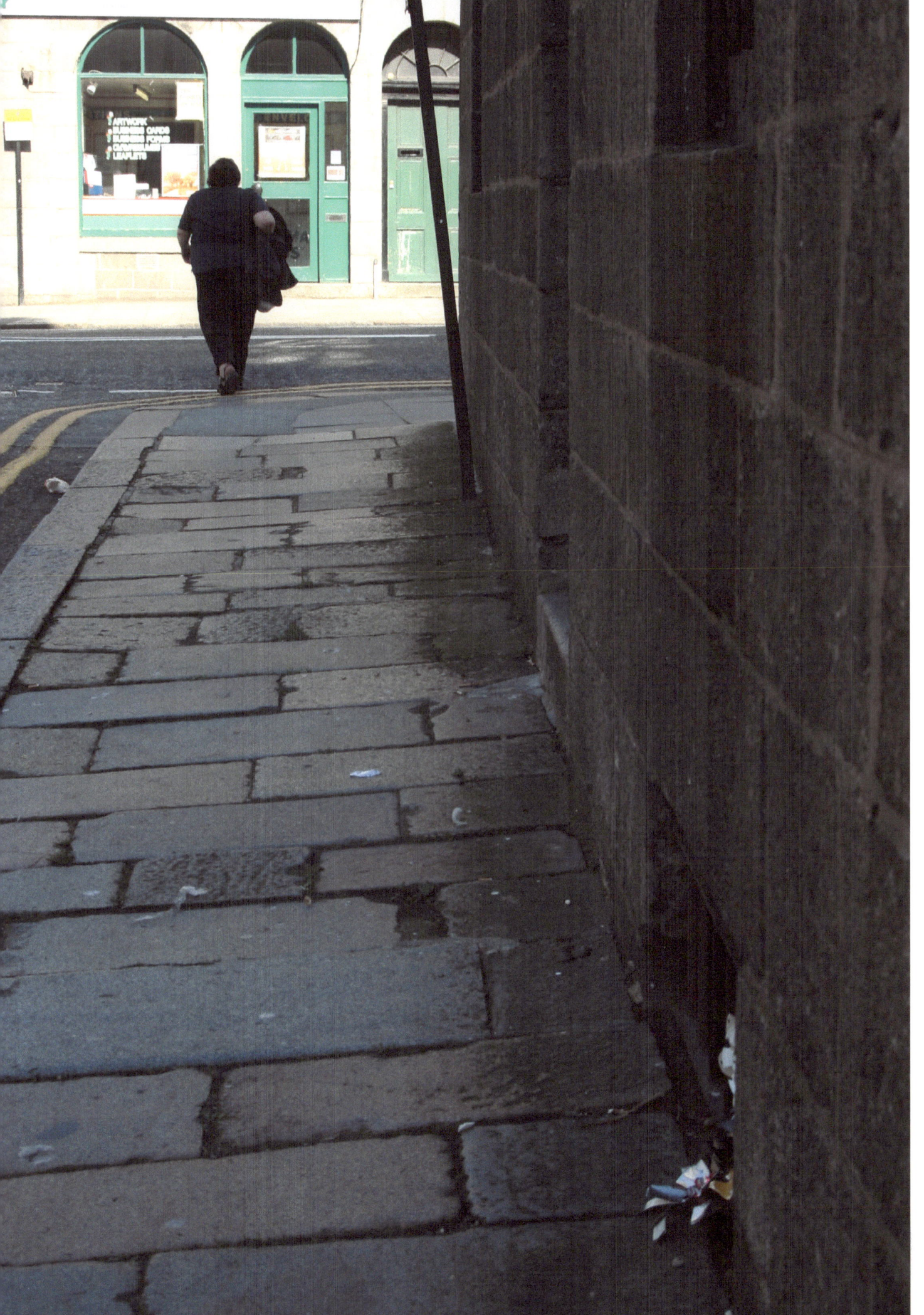

BRETT BLOOM AND BONNIE FORTUNE

The Library of Radiant Optimism for Let's Re-Make the World

We started the library as a way to gather, look at, and catalog a groundswell of optimistic and visionary activities in the late 1960s and early 1970s. We had discussions about the similarities between a handful of books we knew of, and the culture of Mess Hall, an experimental cultural center in Chicago that we have both been active in for over three years. Mess Hall is organized around an "economy of generosity," freely sharing information and materials. The books are important precursors to Mess Hall, embracing the grassroots exchange of information and themes of self and community empowerment. These books are often, but not always, written from the counter-culture. Their authors were interested in communicating their direct experience as it related to their experiments for living in harmony with the natural landscape, building sustainable communities, and so on. We were excited to read about practical applications of optimistic ideas for radical change, and to continue putting our own ideas into this tradition.

There are parallels between the cultural and political climate of the 1970s and current global conditions. However, we feel that an important difference is in the absence of a massive counter-cultural movement for change. We face many of the same problems – large-scale ideological wars, energy crises, environmental devastation, destructive global capitalism and more. The hopeful quality of these books encourages us in developing a movement of our own, in the form of how-to manuals with the explicit intent of building a new society of optimistic resistance. This gives us hope as we go through our experiments; some things will not work, but the diversity of investigations in living creatively means that more possibilities for intelligent solutions will appear.

We will add these and more books from around the world, and our own projects to the history, and are currently looking for similar books and projects.

[Brett Bloom and Bonnie Fortune]

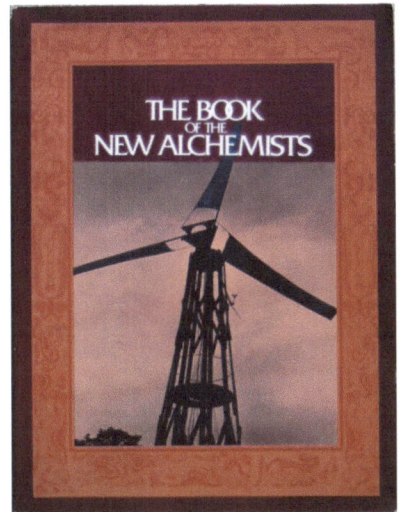

The Book of the New Alchemists, Edited by Nancy Jack Todd, E. P. Dutton, 1977, 174 pages, paperback, ISBN: 0-525-47465-X

"A few years ago, a small group of artists, scientists, and thinkers concerned about the rapidity of the Earth's destruction and the impending disintegration of social and moral values, joined together to form an organization with a name of peculiar significance for our time – The New Alchemy Institute."

The Book of the New Alchemists is a document of a living experiment begun in 1969 by a group of people concerned with what they saw as an approaching ecological crisis. Eschewing the unsustainable in the dominant culture, they chose to drop out and create a micro-culture and economy with their own radical methods. This book is a document of their optimistic experiment in self-reliance.

We like this book because it has important analyses of the dangers of pesticide use on crops, beginner's accounts of composting, poems, manifestos, and a chapter on women and ecology. It provides loads of information on how to build your own bio-shelters and aquaculture systems. Their analysis of the human relationship to the earth, presented in a personal and direct manner are interspersed with art and poetry to make for an engaging and unifying experience.

The New Alchemists created and documented their use of "Living Machines." Based on the environment of wetlands, Living Machines are sophisticated micro-ecosystems that do a variety of functions simultaneously. The Living Machines process human waste as food for microorganisms in water containers, the waste of the microorganisms serve as food for vegetables and fish that humans can eat. The New Alchemists used aquaculture and created bio-shelters (one example is pictured on page 3) – systems that people lived with and in – that were sensitive to the needs of the plants, animals, and environment that everything shares. This is interesting because it places humans back into the ecological cycle rather than trying to manufacture or design a solution to a problem derived from the very sources of the problem.

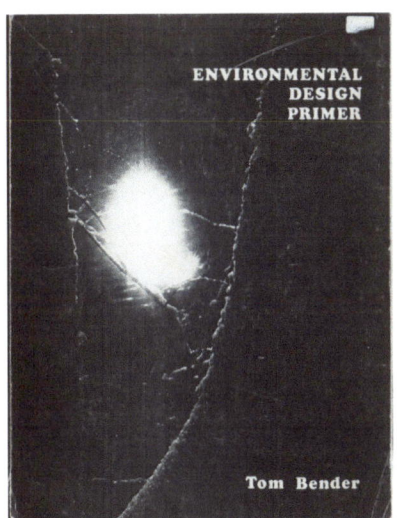

Environmental Design Primer, By Tom Bender, Schocken Books, 1976, 207 pages, paperback, ISBN: 0805205136

Tom Bender is an architect who was at the forefront of the sustainability movement. This book, published in 1973, is a scrapbook collection of musings, quotes, images, and philosophies culled from a myriad of sources. The book is a starting place for Bender's personal investigation of how we can live lightly, in harmony with the land. The book is a relevant document of thoughts in the environmental and sustainability movements of today, and it is easy to get lost in the wandering collage-like style of the book's design.

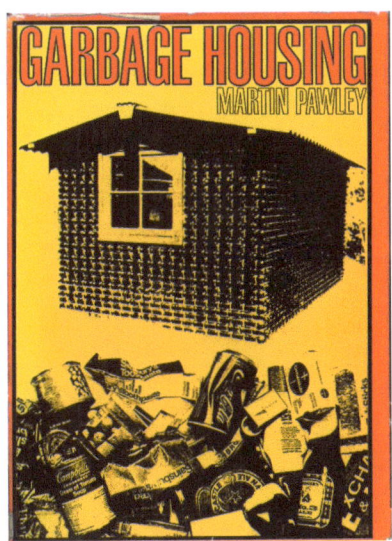

Garbage Housing, By Martin Pawley, Krieger Publishing Company, 1975, 118 pages, hardcover, ISBN: 0470672781

Industrialized global capitalism has failed to provide affordable housing for everyone. Yet, it is possible to get carbonated soft drinks in aluminum cans into the hands of millions of people worldwide. Martin Pawley looks at this conundrum and rightfully asks how we could let this happen. He demands that we ask more of the consumer goods we make, that we learn from them to address all the problems that our consumer culture has generated. His solution to housing crises is to build dwellings out of garbage – to design our garbage to better accommodate the housing needs of those left out of consumer society's benefits. This book is captivating. It investigates the use of cast-off materials in the slums of Chile. An entire chapter is devoted to the Heineken World Bottle (WOBO). In 1960, Alfred Heineken created the WOBO – interlocking and self-aligning bottles – to hold his well-known beer for Caribbean consumers. Once the bottle was emptied, it could be used to build a shelter. The WOBO demonstrates what Pawley refers to as "secondary use," that is, everything we design should be made with further uses in mind.

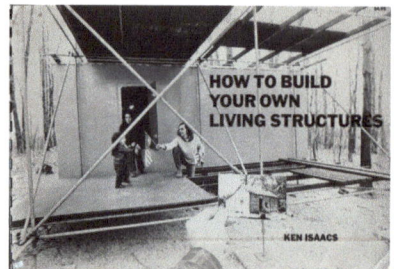

How To Build Your Own Living Structures, By Ken Isaacs, Harmony Books, 1974, 136 pages, spiral bound, ASIN: B0006C58MM

This book is a beautiful guide about how to make a variety of flexible experimental indoor interiors, storage units, and a microhouse. The microhouse is a flexible creation of architect Ken Isaacs. The modular design is based on stacked tetrahedrons, which can be moved in and around each other providing shelter and dividing living space in a creative way. The book gives you step-by-step instructions with plans for many different versions of Isaac's original designs interspersed with ideas about simplicity, and getting rid of our personal possessions. The book is type written and spiral bound in a nice Do-It-Yourself aesthetic, and Isaacs writes in a genial manner as if he were sitting across the table from you. He muses on the philosophical meanings of surplus and uses the designs as a means of addressing life as a whole; a simple place to raise a family and house extended family that has a low impact on the surrounding natural environment.

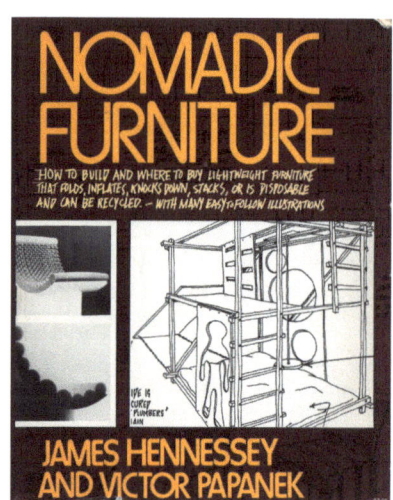

Nomadic Furniture, By Victor Papanek, Pantheon, 1973, 149 pages, paperback, ISBN: 039470228X

Nomadic Furniture is a simple how-to book based on conscious design and creative materials. A design professor and an industrial designer wrote the book for those with a modern nomadic lifestyle. Much of the designs in this book are made with cardboard, light wood, or innovatively reused materials. All the designs are economical and creative. The authors relate their own experiences with the use of the designs, as well as how one might incorporate them in day-to-day life.

The book covers everything from how to make a bed to building a child's car seat from cardboard. It provides detailed measurements and descriptions of the tools you will need to build the items in the book.

Nomadic Furniture 2, By James Hennessey, Pantheon, 1974, paperback, 153 pages, ISBN: 978-0394706382

The second volume of Nomadic Furniture is every bit as engaging as the first. This volume contains projects from hanging lamps to kitchen tools to various kinds of folding and adjustable chairs. Highlights include instructions on how to make playgrounds from old car tires as well as elaborate and abstract rope and wood tree houses for children. The authors of both volumes want readers to make the projects in the books as well as use them for inspiration on original creative projects. They even provide many blank pages at the end of each volume to make your own notes.

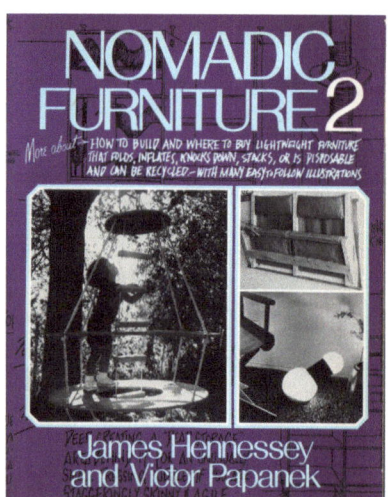

Pedal Power in Work, Leisure, and Transportation, By James C. McCullagh, Rodale Press, 1977, 144 pages, ISBN: 978-0878571789

This book is a fascinating overview of the history of pedal power, used in building ancient monuments, personal transportation, pumping water from wells and pumping air for deep sea divers, grinding grain, spinning yarn, and more. The authors present the background material as inspiration for modern applications. They ask us to return to simpler technology to do some of today's mechanized tasks. To this end, there are many detailed plans on how to adapt electrically powered tools and devices to pedal power. With the author's instructions, you can make a pedal-powered television or generate electricity for your home, and there are at least two varieties of pedal-powered washing machines. More whimsical are the instructions for making a bicycle that you can ride on railroad tracks. However, there are some rather ridiculous ideas too, the most absurd being the two-person pedal-powered plow. You can see the futility and inefficiency of the device in the illustrations. The varieties of creative uses, practical and impractical, for energy generated from pedal power make this book so terrific.

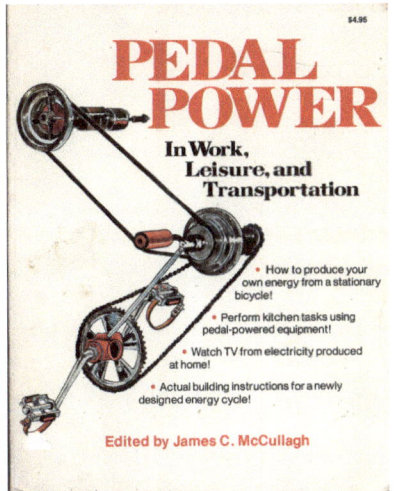

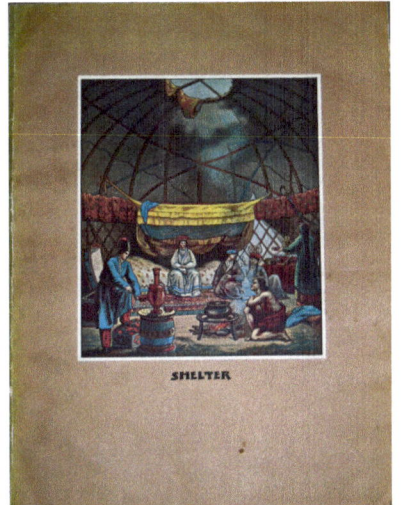

Shelter, By Lloyd Kahn, Shelter Publications, 1973, 176 pages, paperback, ISBN: 0394709918

Shelter is a catalog of construction methods of living spaces from around the world. The book focuses on homes that are creatively designed, often highlighting nomadic structures, or structures that consider the ecology of place. Its pages include everything from the unbelievable Cones of Cappadocia in Turkey – homes carved into dramatic cones of rock that jut out of the earth – to the Yurts of nomadic people from Mongolia to Iran. It is both an anthropological investigation of how people house themselves and a call to live closer to one's immediate environment. The book is a great collection of images but also includes articles with environmental builders, including tips on using found or recycled materials in the creation of your own habitat. Famous hippie settlements like Drop City, and houses built onto the chassis of trucks or buses for easily driving from place to place, are well documented in this book. There is a lot of information about building geodesic domes – this book is clearly inspired by Buckminster Fuller and the Whole Earth Catalog (biannual from 1968-1972 and sporadically until 1998, "Its purposes were to provide education and 'access to tools' in order that the reader could 'find his own inspiration, shape his own environment, and share his adventure with who[m]ever is interested.' Wikipedia) It is an inspiring book, showing that it is possible to live with greater variety and intentionality, addressing our responsibilities to the environment with our habitats.

Spiritual Midwifery, By Ina May Gaskin, Book Publishing Company, 1976, 480 pages, paperback, ISBN: 1570671044

Spiritual Midwifery, now in its fourth printing, is a must read for students of midwifery but it is also an influential history of the counter-culture. Ina May Gaskin and her husband Stephen Gaskin are founding members of The Farm in Summertown, TN, one of the longest running communes in the United States. The Farm was founded in 1971, Ina May published Spiritual Midwifery in 1975 to document the beginning of the Farm and the development of a successful out of hospital birth center, one of the first in the US. The book describes how the Farm was settled and how soon after there was a need for safe and secure medical care for pregnant and birthing women. The Farm Midwives learned how to be midwives out of necessity. An understanding local doctor aided them along with their education. The Midwives have gone on to deliver thousands of babies and are still practicing today.

The majority of the book is a collection of birth stories from the women of the Farm. The fourth edition has added birth stories from the Old Amish Families near the Farm whom some of the Midwives worked with, and birth stories from people who came to the Farm just to give birth. The book also includes a practical section for midwifery students with how-to skills infused with the Farm philosophy of home birth.

Ina May's writing makes this book special, particularly in the way she frames the material. Although she never set out to be a midwife, she pays close attention to the way words affect how women perceive not only labor, but also their bodies in general. In the book, she weaves a powerful history of a group of people creating their own place in the world, calmly and peacefully, and how communication through specific language and touch plays a vital part in the success of their endeavors. There are also amazing photos of women giving birth.

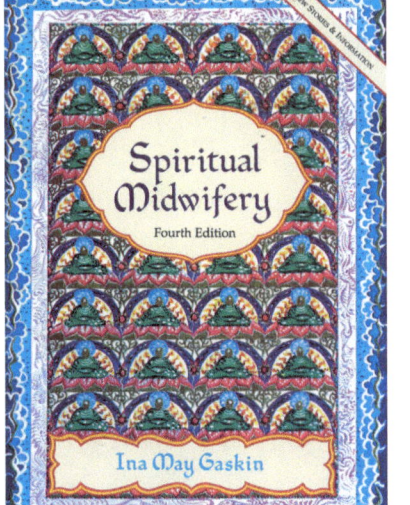

MARJOLIJN DIJKMAN

'Theatrum Orbis Terrarum'

Theatrum Orbis Terrarum is a collection of photographs taken by the artist during her travels all over the world. Intended partly as research material to develop site-specific works and partly as a personal investigation, a selection of this archive relating to Adaptation is presented here in this catalogue. Together with Julie Peeters a series of publications and printed matter are being produced.

While confirming Dijkman's interest in the nature of public space, this work also attempts to map connections and similarities among different places in the world. Dijkman takes inspiration from Ortelius' Theatrum Orbis Terrarum (Theatre of the World), which is considered the first atlas in the modern sense. But other than Ortelius, Dijkman categorises the images according to personal criteria instead of objective and fixed categories. Those categories, ordered by the gesture how the situations appear, are subject to shifts and expansion, influenced by new explorations and encounters.

Theatrum orbis Terrarum. A selection of ongoing research
Photography Marjolijn Dijkman
Design Julie Peeters
Distributed by Jan van Eyck Academy, Peacock Visual Arts,
Bonner Kunstverrein; order online at marjolijndijkman.com
ISBN 978-0-9555524-0-3

List of categories of the archive

Abandon	Confuse	Exclude	Maintain	Provide
Abuse	Connect	Explain	Mark	Refuse
Adapt	Console	Fetishize	Measure	Regenerate
Adjust	Construct	Flatten	Mirror	Remain
Adopt	Contact	Gather	Mobilize	Repel
Announce	Contain	Give Shelter	Mock	Reveal
Apologize	Control	Globalize	Neglect	Seduce
Appropriate	Correct	Grasp	Obey	Simulate
Assemble	Cover	Guide	Obstruct	Struggle
Avert	Demarcate	Hide	Occupy	Suffocate
Botch	Demonstrate	Honor	Open up	Support
Burst	Depend	Illuminate	Oppress	Surprise
Camouflage	Direct	Imagine	Order	Surrender
Carry	Disguise	Imitate	Penetrate	Tempt
Celebrate	Displace	Impress	Perforate	Torture
Censor	Display	Indicate	Perform	Turn inside out
Cheer up	Divide	Interrupt	Privatize	Turn pale
Civilize	Dramatize	Intertwine	Profit	Wait
Collect	Embrace	Invade	Prohibit	Warn
Compose	Enclose	Invite	Propose	
Conceal	Encourage	Irritate	Protect	
Confront	Erase	Isolate	Protest	

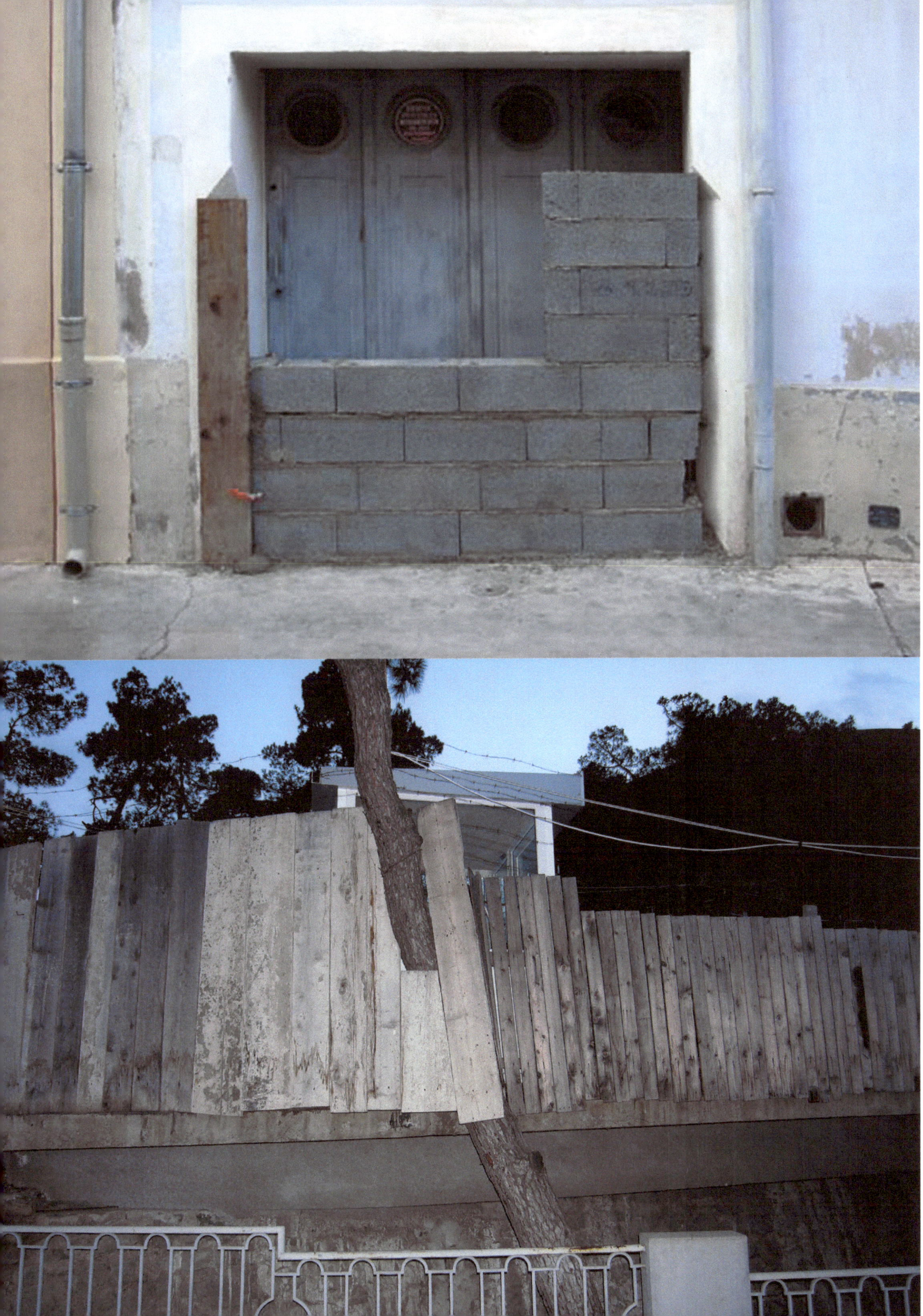

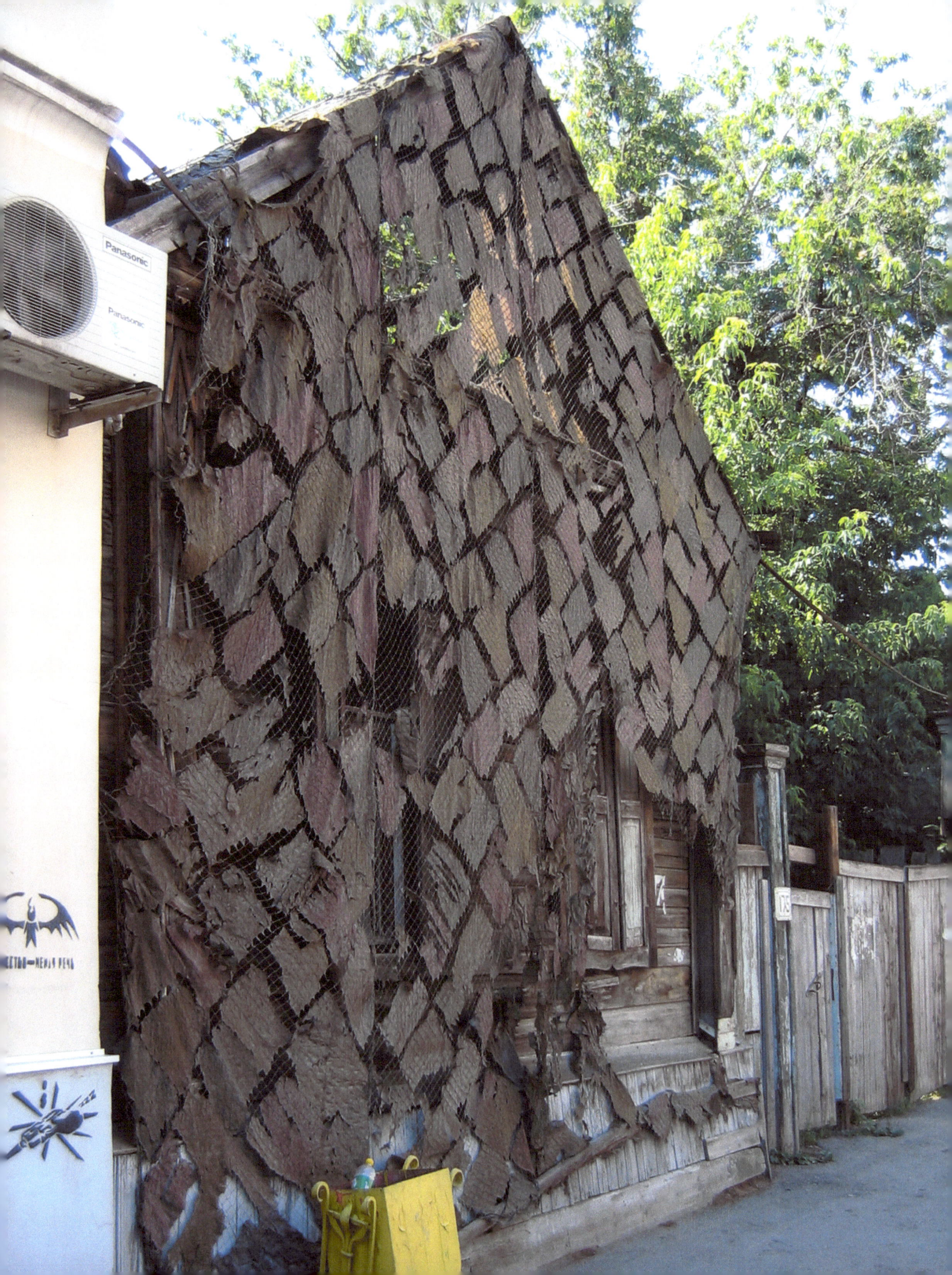

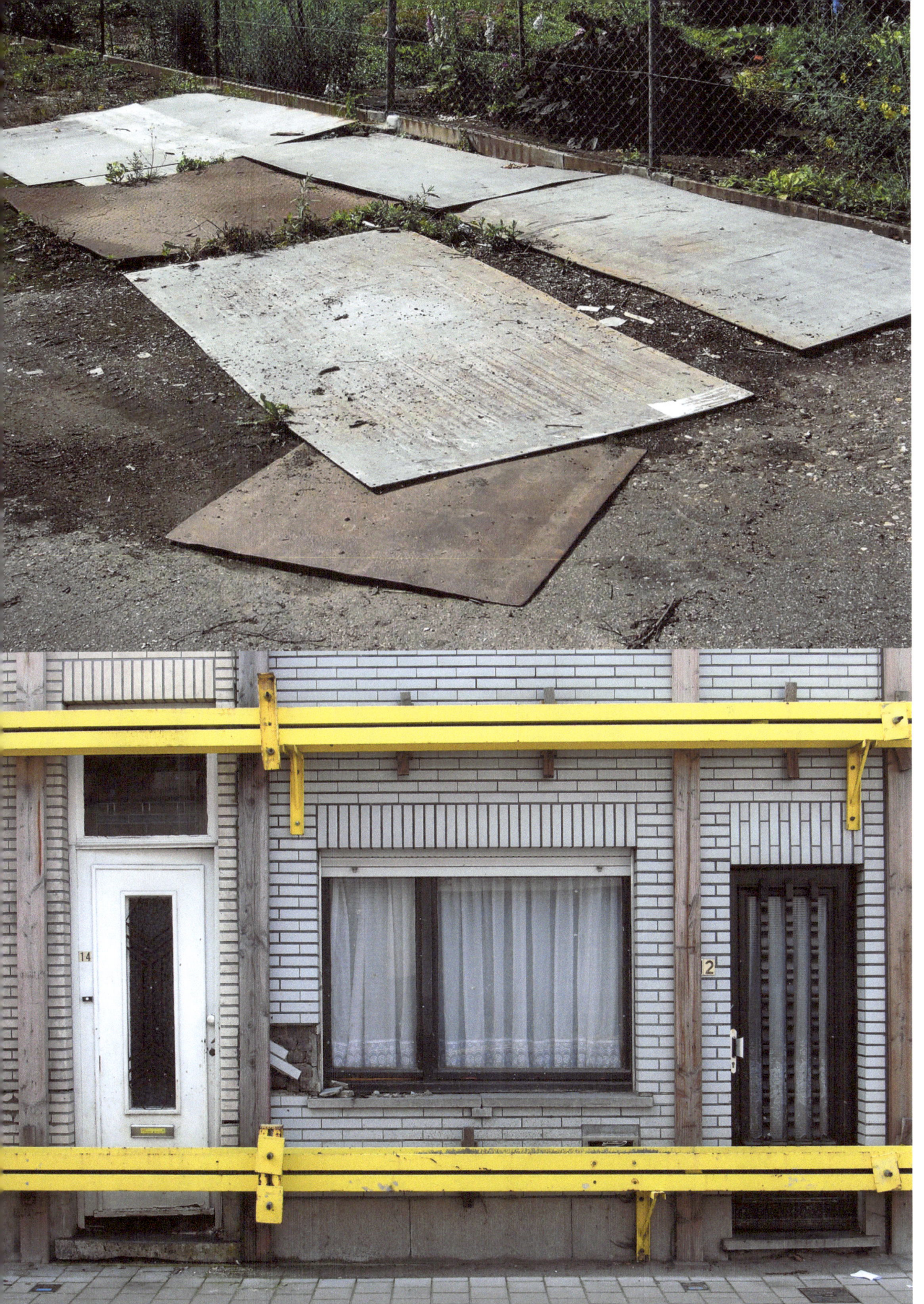

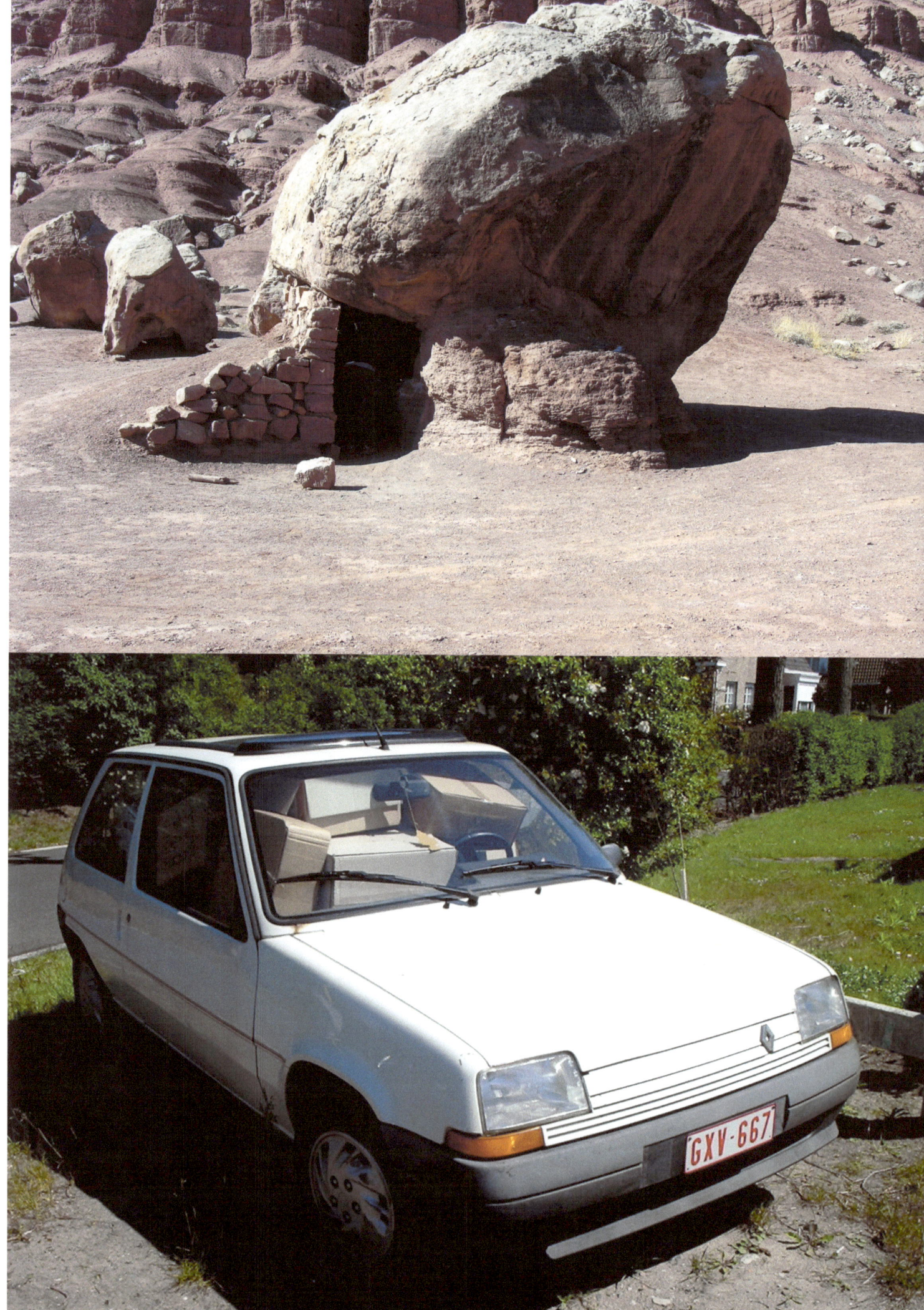

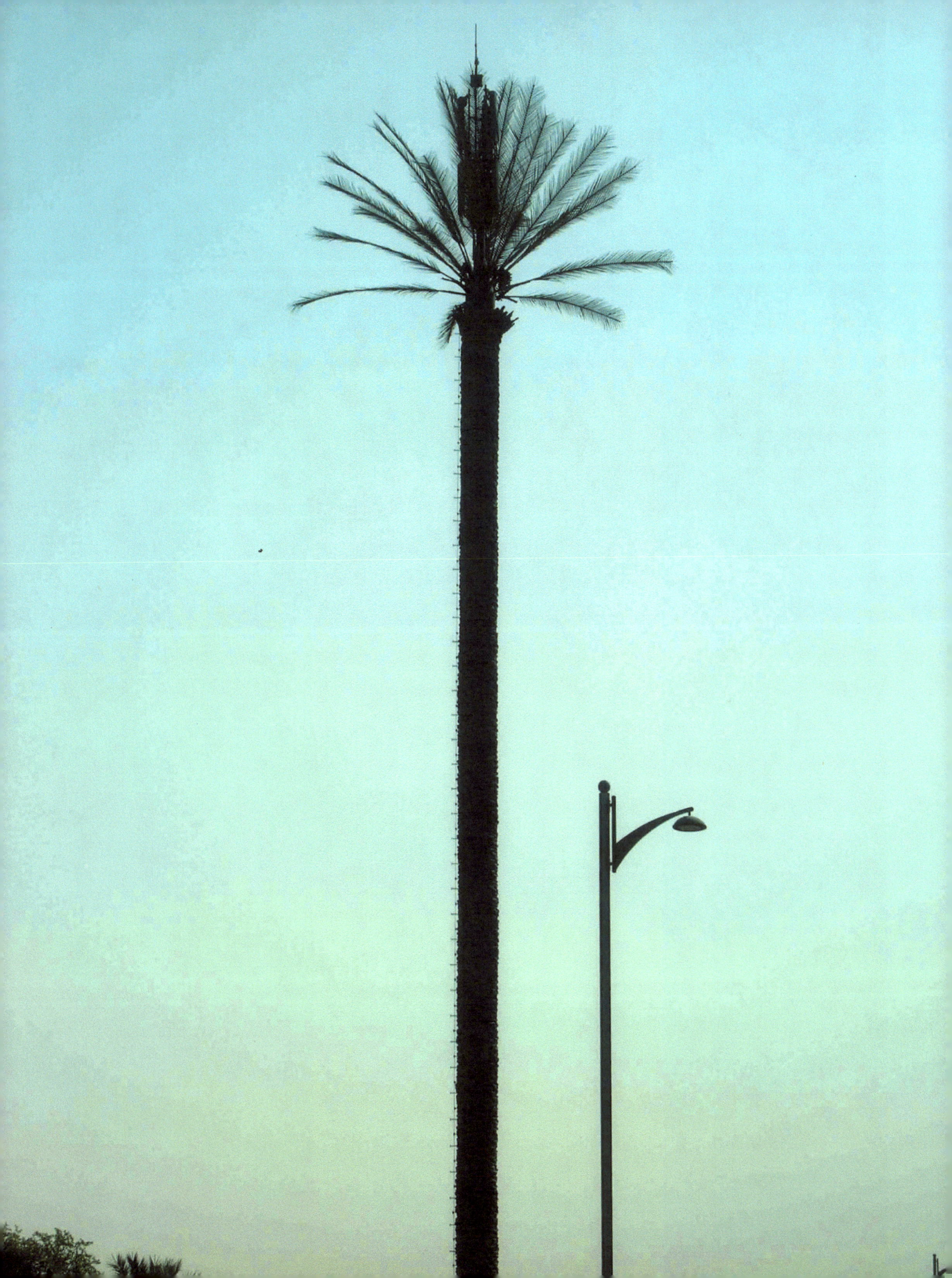

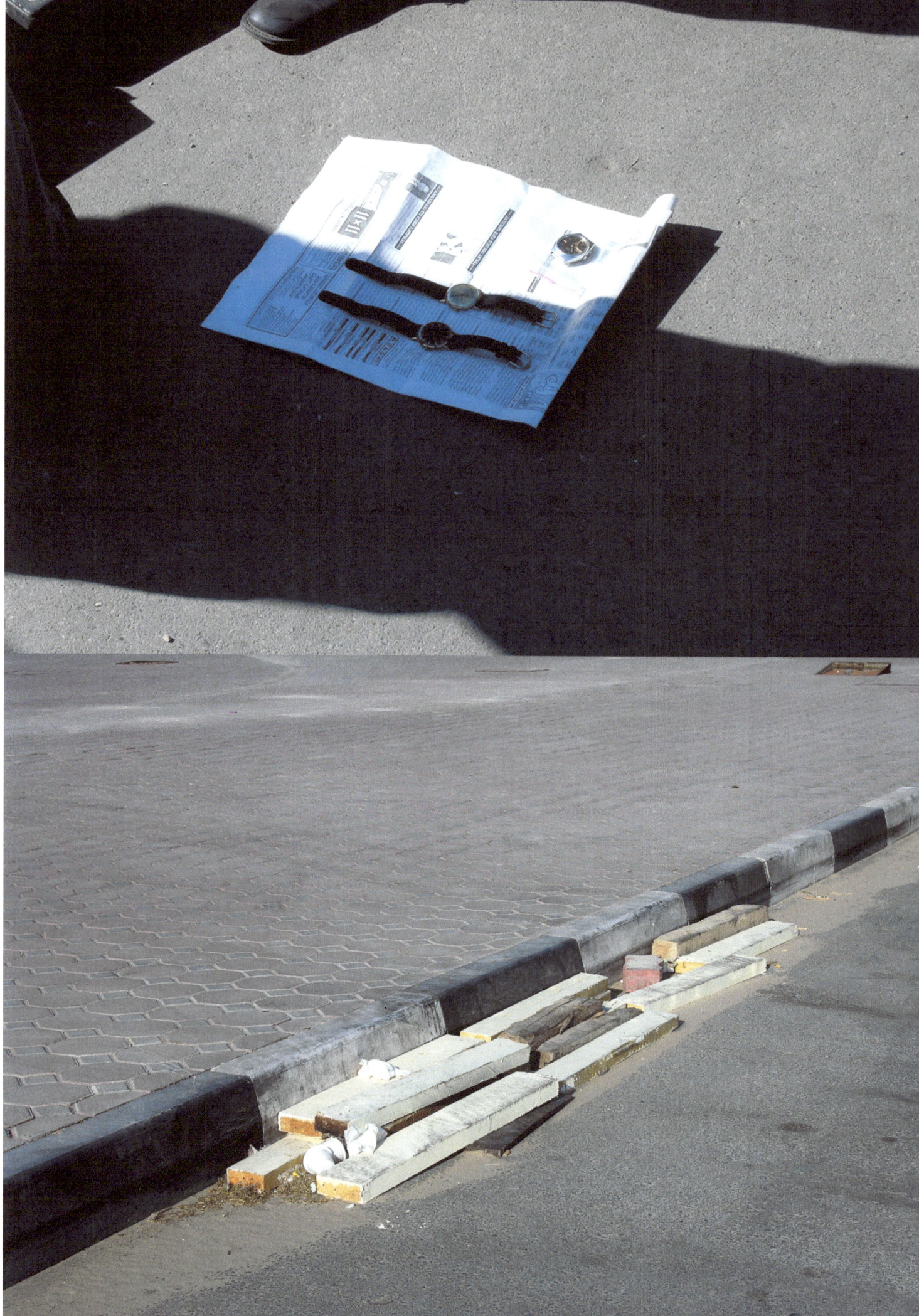

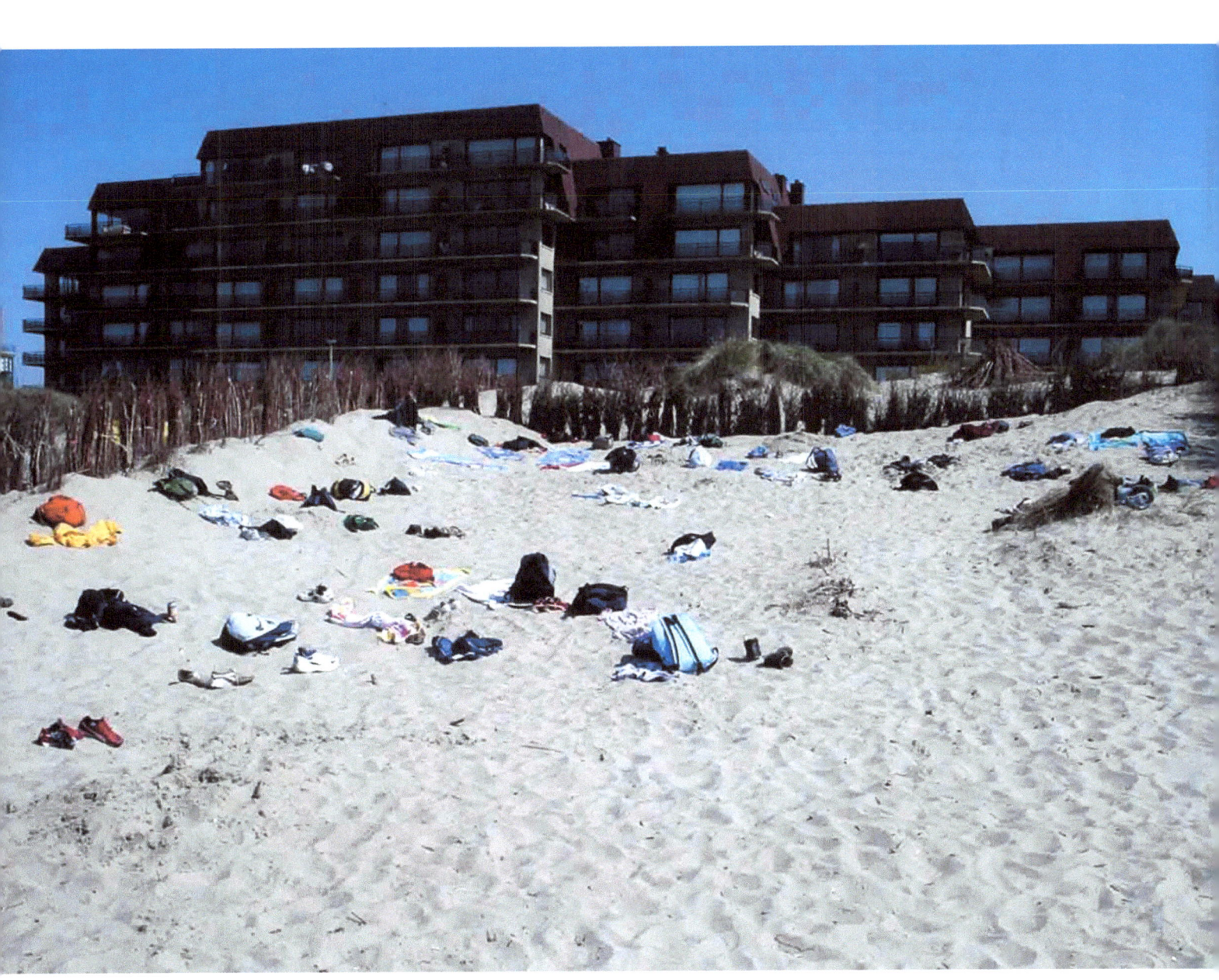

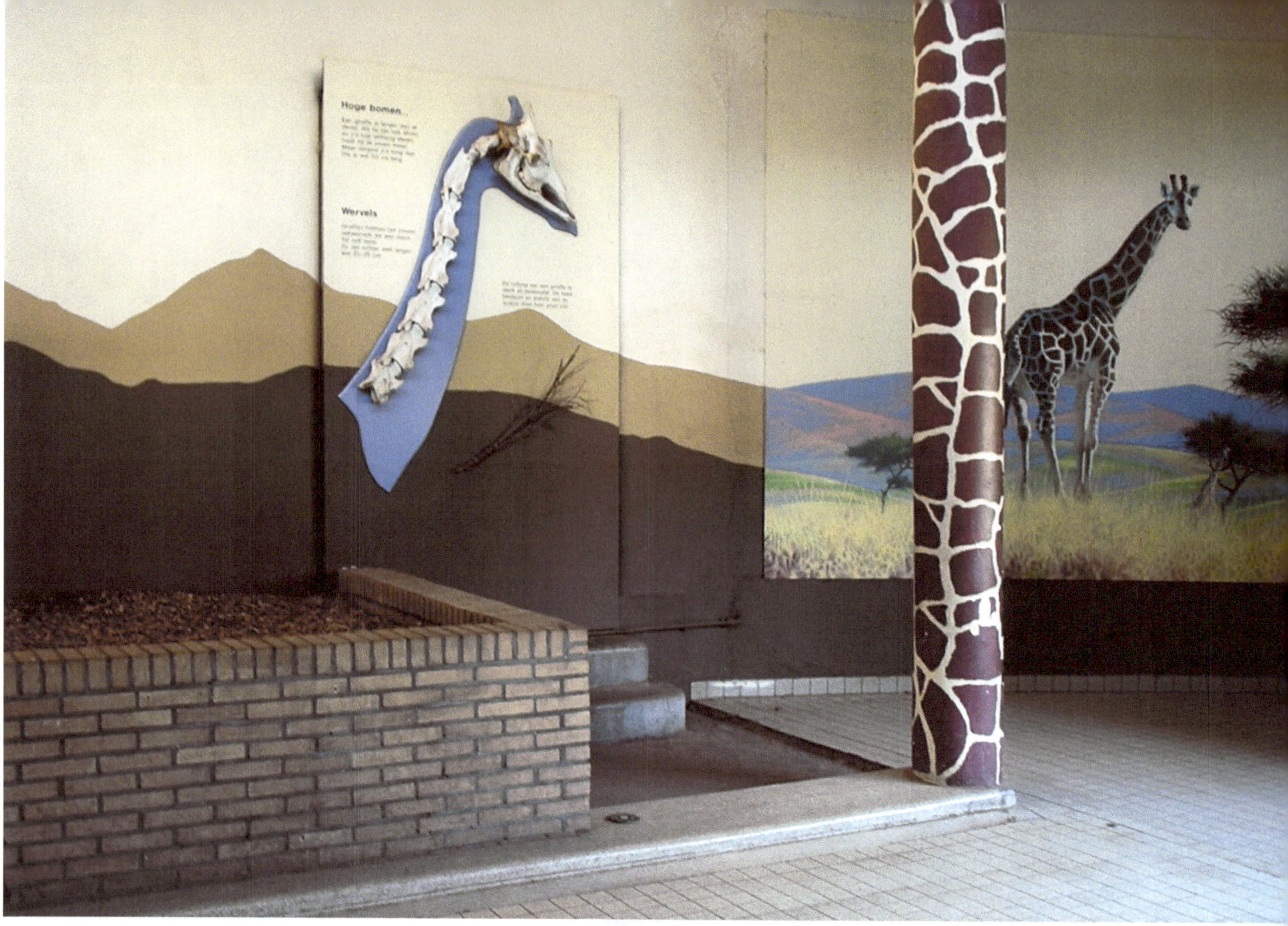

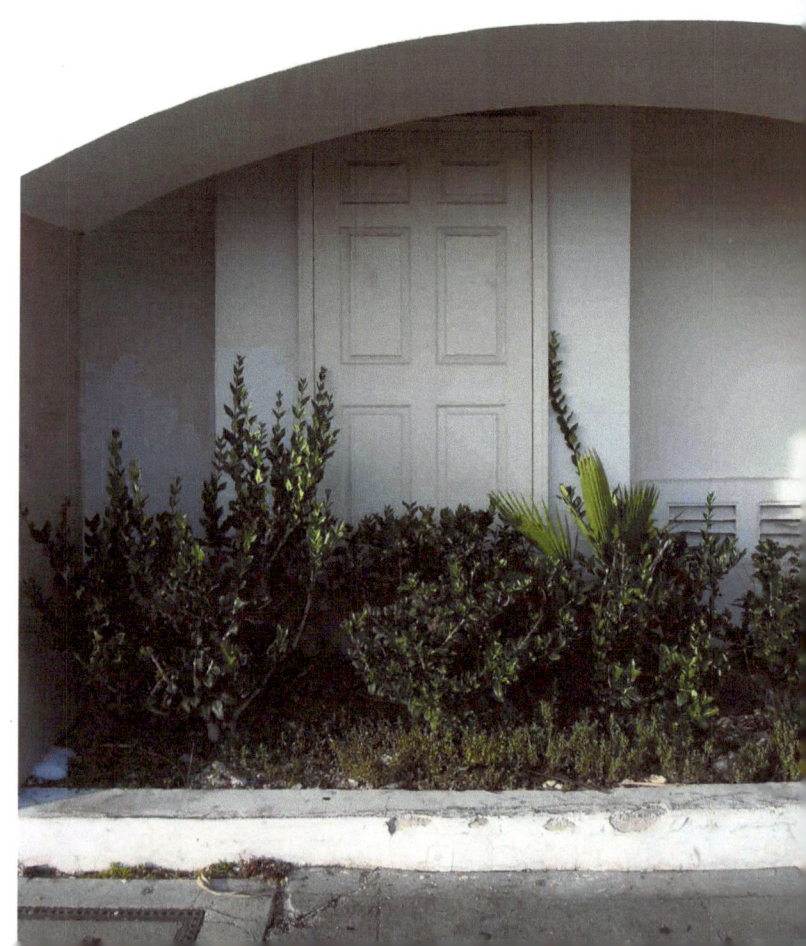

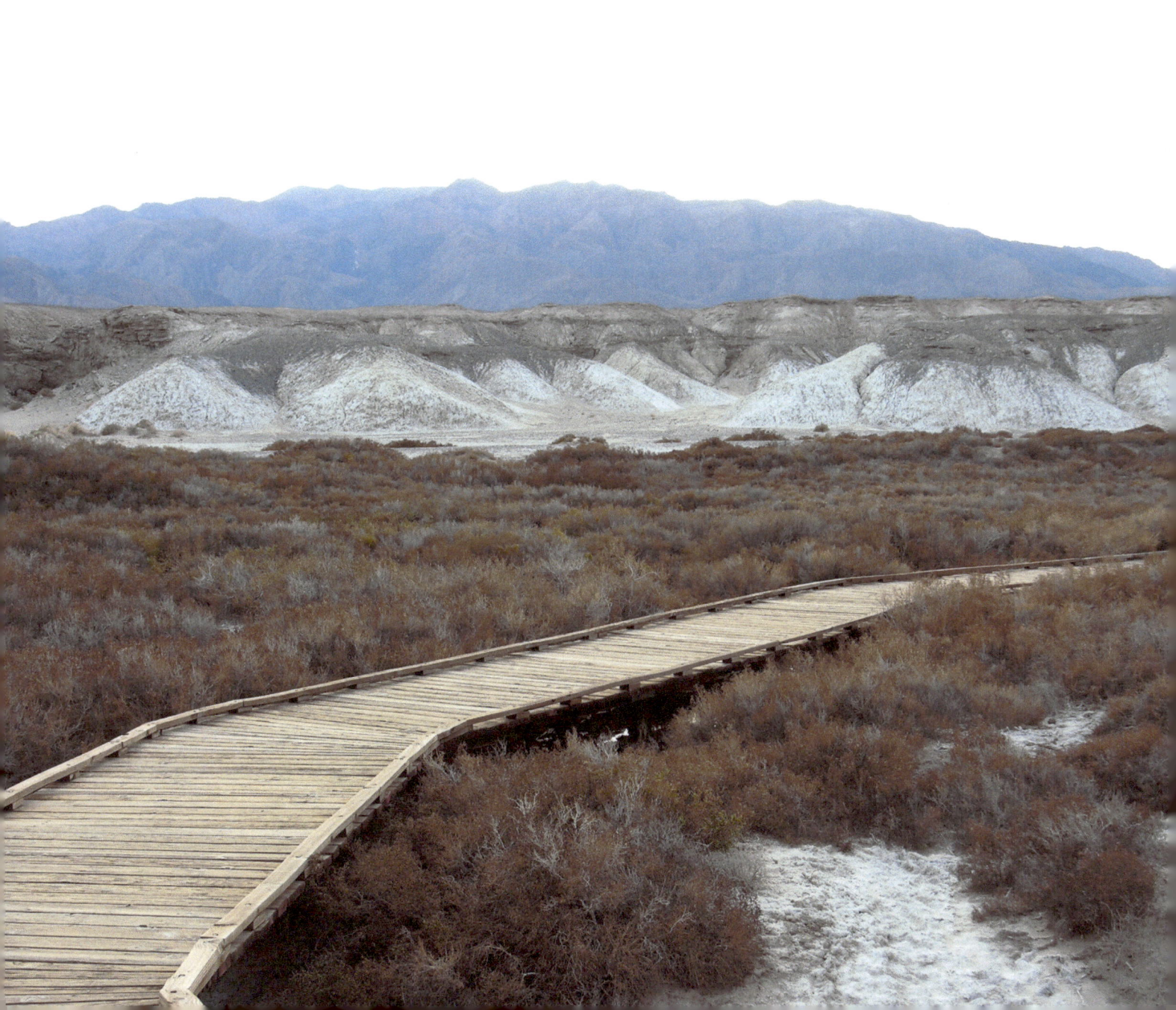

BRAD DOWNEY

Trouble Brewing

During his visit to Aberdeen for Adaptation, I was unofficially Brad's minder. I tagged along with him as he worked on the preparation for his heart piece, surveying potential sites and gathering resources. On one particular afternoon we visited the Aberdeen Art Gallery, at that time running the Aberdeen Artists Society exhibition. With the oil company Shell sponsoring the exhibition, in a town world famous for its prominence in the oil business, it is a subject matter on which an artist like Brad has much opinion. Whilst viewing the works, Brad's eye was drawn to the various pieces that had been awarded a commendation by Shell. Actually, he was primarily drawn to the 'commended' signs themselves. Considering that one piece Brad had displayed in his contribution to Adaptation was an image playing with the Shell motif, it is easy to see why. With no human or electronic surveillant present, and against my initial reservation, Brad calmly removed a 'commended' tag from the wall. Leaving the lumps of white tack that had solely held the tag in place, Brad slipped it into his pocket and sauntered away from the crime scene. I must say that even I saw the funny side as we made our way up Schoolhill, joking about what had just occured. Though I left most of my concern behind in the gallery, I still felt that this minor misdemeanor was a precursor to something on a far larger scale...

[Brian Ross]

hell

sHELL, 1999
Location: Atlanta, Georgia
Materials: a hammer and balls
Duration: Unknown

My Trouble with Brad

While making our way to the site of what would very soon
become Brad Downey's latest work, a seagull pooped on me.
Though this is a common occurrence in Aberdeen, it was one
that I had, perhaps unfairly, managed to avoid in the six odd
years I have lived in this city. Craig Barrowman, camera man,
quipped that he had caught the incident on film. Brad tried to
lighten my solemn mood; " They say that's a sign of good luck",
he remarked. Somehow I felt otherwise...

At around 9 o'clock the previous night I had been lingering in
the same spot with Brad and a projector. Whilst I kept guard
of the projector, Brad monkeyed his way up the scaffolding
opposite and marked out the large heart shape being beamed
onto the red tarpaulin that was his canvas, so to speak. It was a
surreal event for me, the highlight being a colourful discussion
on immigrant labourers with an inebriated gentleman who
insisted he was not a racist, though his terminology seemed to
hark back to the colonial days. Regardless, the operation went
without difficulty. I assumed that the following night would run
as smoothly.

With cameras rolling and tension mounting, Brad Downey
began the final assault. Pulling up his grey hoodie and with his
weapons of choice in a carrier bag stuffed in his pocket, Brad
pulled himself up to the first level of walkway (with in-the-field
camera operator Eva Merz capturing the action close up) and
looked to the outline he had marked the night before. I manned
a camera we had borrowed from a friend, taking shots roughly a
minute apart... Well, what I perceived as a minute. The tension
was getting to me, and I could feel the sweat running down
my spine. The cutting of the tarpaulin was smoother than I
had expected. It was, for me, a beautiful sight as this immense
heart took form. Passers-by glanced up at the spectacle. I
heard later that one had remarked on the romantic resonance
of the image, that "he must really love his girlfriend..."; another
bystander commented on the trouble he was going to get into.

Quite true, really.

Bundling up the fallen red material that had drifted down to the
road quite gently, Brad was apprehended by the owner of the
building, who just happened to be inside of it while this had all
taken place. He proceeded to call the owner of the scaffolding
and (rather expensive) tarpaulin, Graeme Cheyne. He was,
unsurprisingly, vexed at this discovery. Brad pleaded his case,
as I crossed the road to be present to this unfolding drama. At
Brad's request, we made our way to Peacock to validate the
account he had given to the tarpaulin's owner.

Though it had been tense at times, the evening of Thursday,
10th of May ended on a highly positive note. Brad commented
on the success of the piece, and seemed to be both exhilarated
and relieved. A cup of coffee was greatly deserved as he wound
down after the drama had subsided. I personally am truly
grateful to have been part of this event, and I feel that such
statements are greatly needed these days. I would like to thank
Brad for letting me be part of this achievement.

...I still think he's trouble, though.

[Brian Ross]

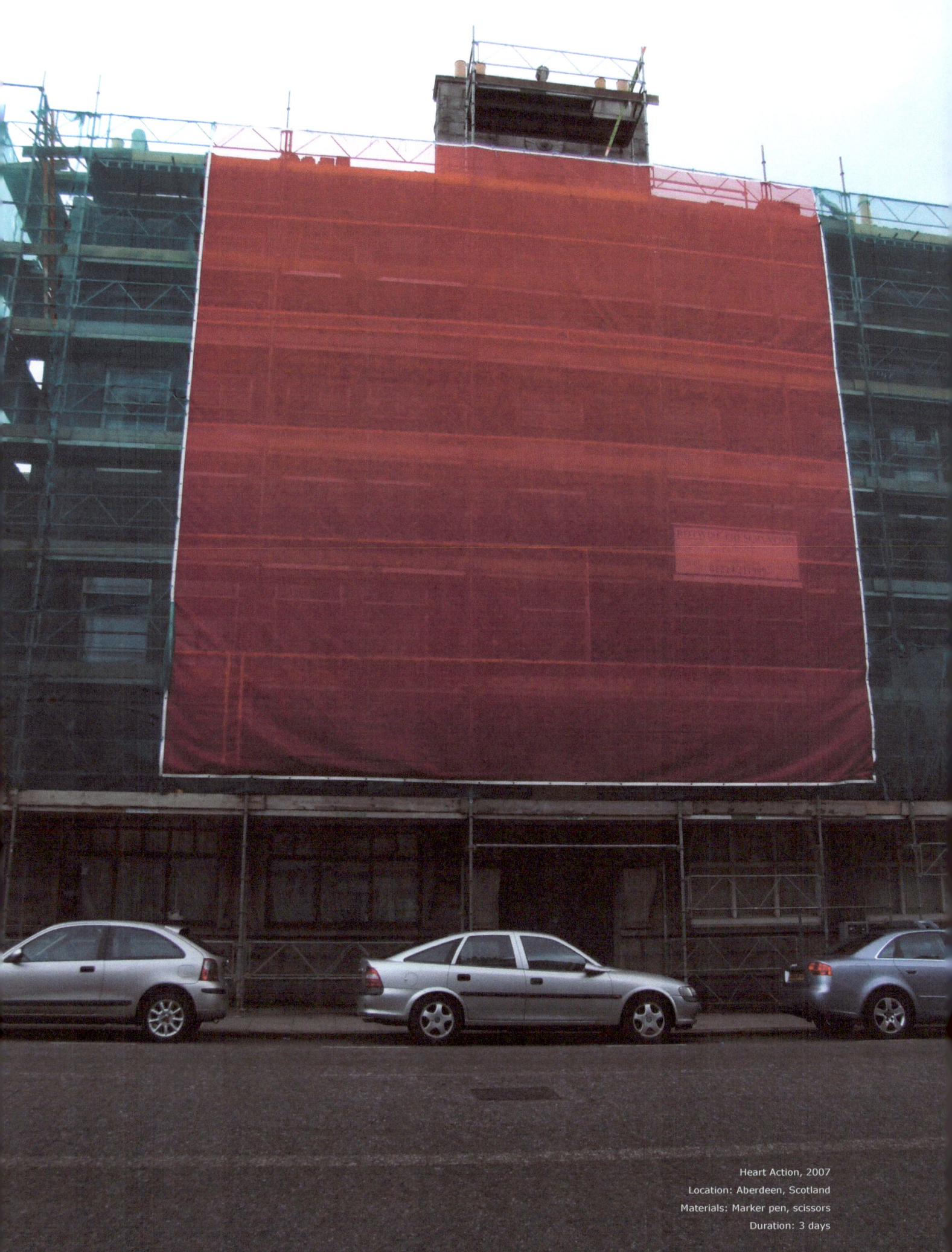

Heart Action, 2007
Location: Aberdeen, Scotland
Materials: Marker pen, scissors
Duration: 3 days

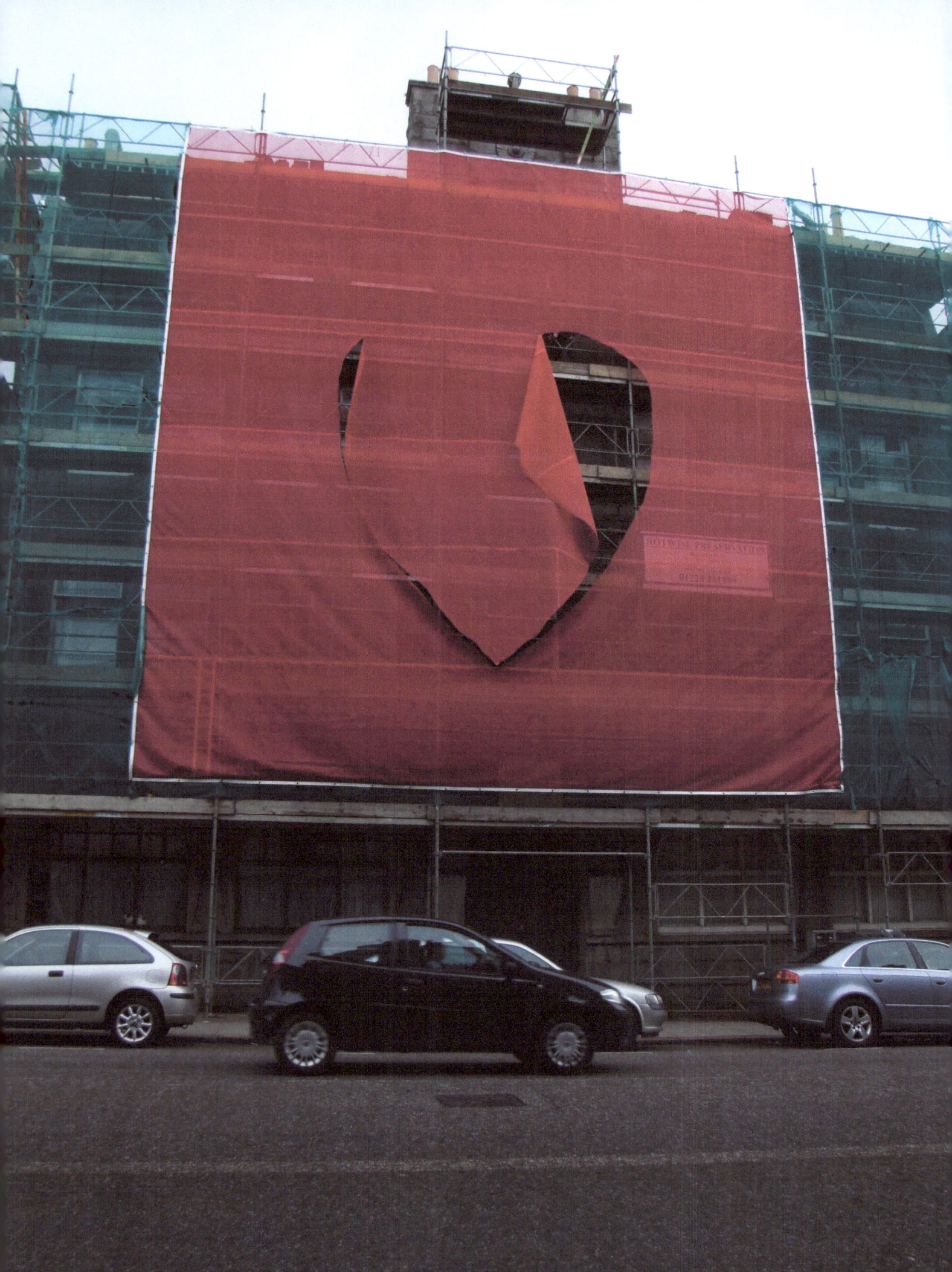

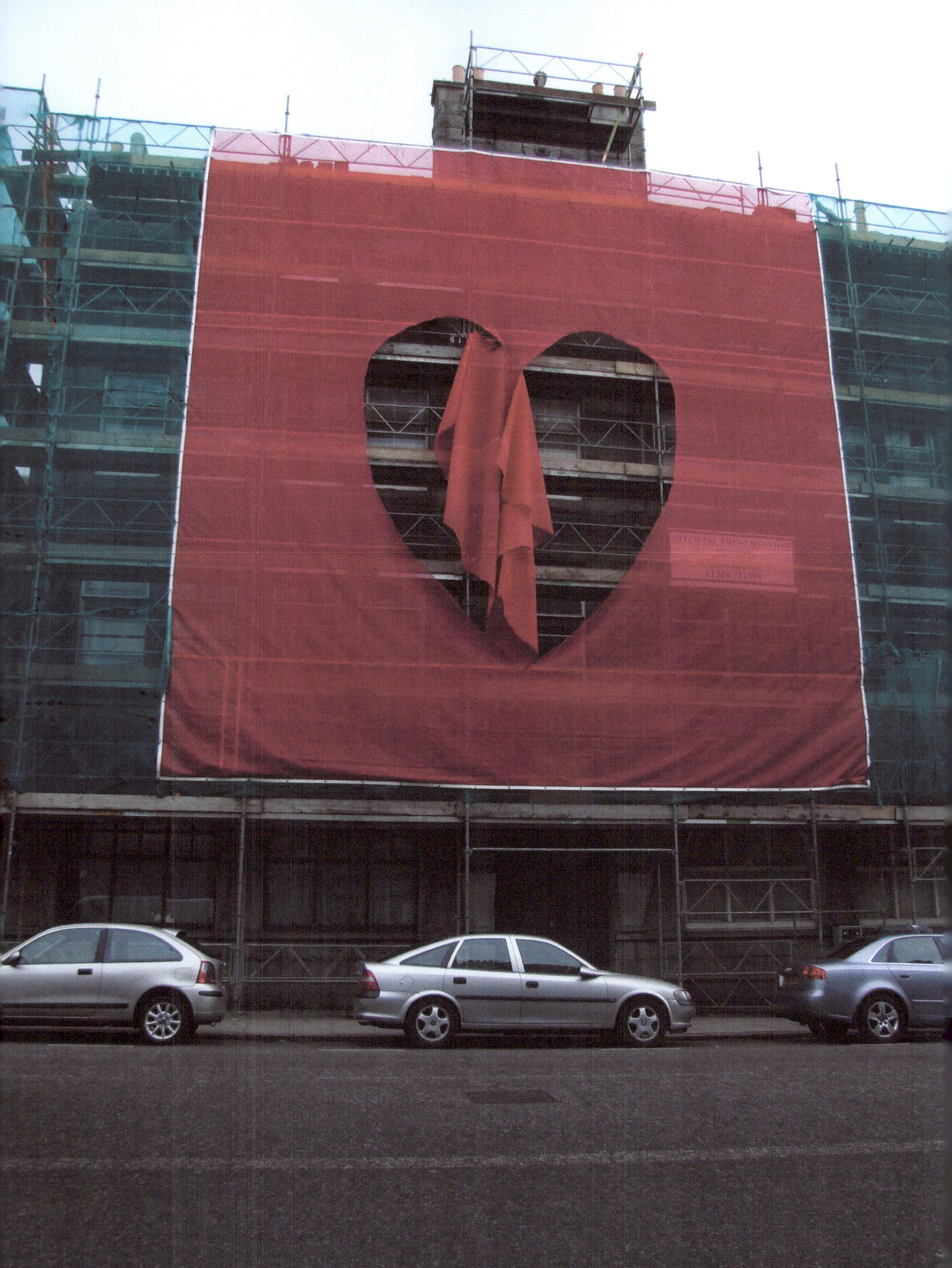

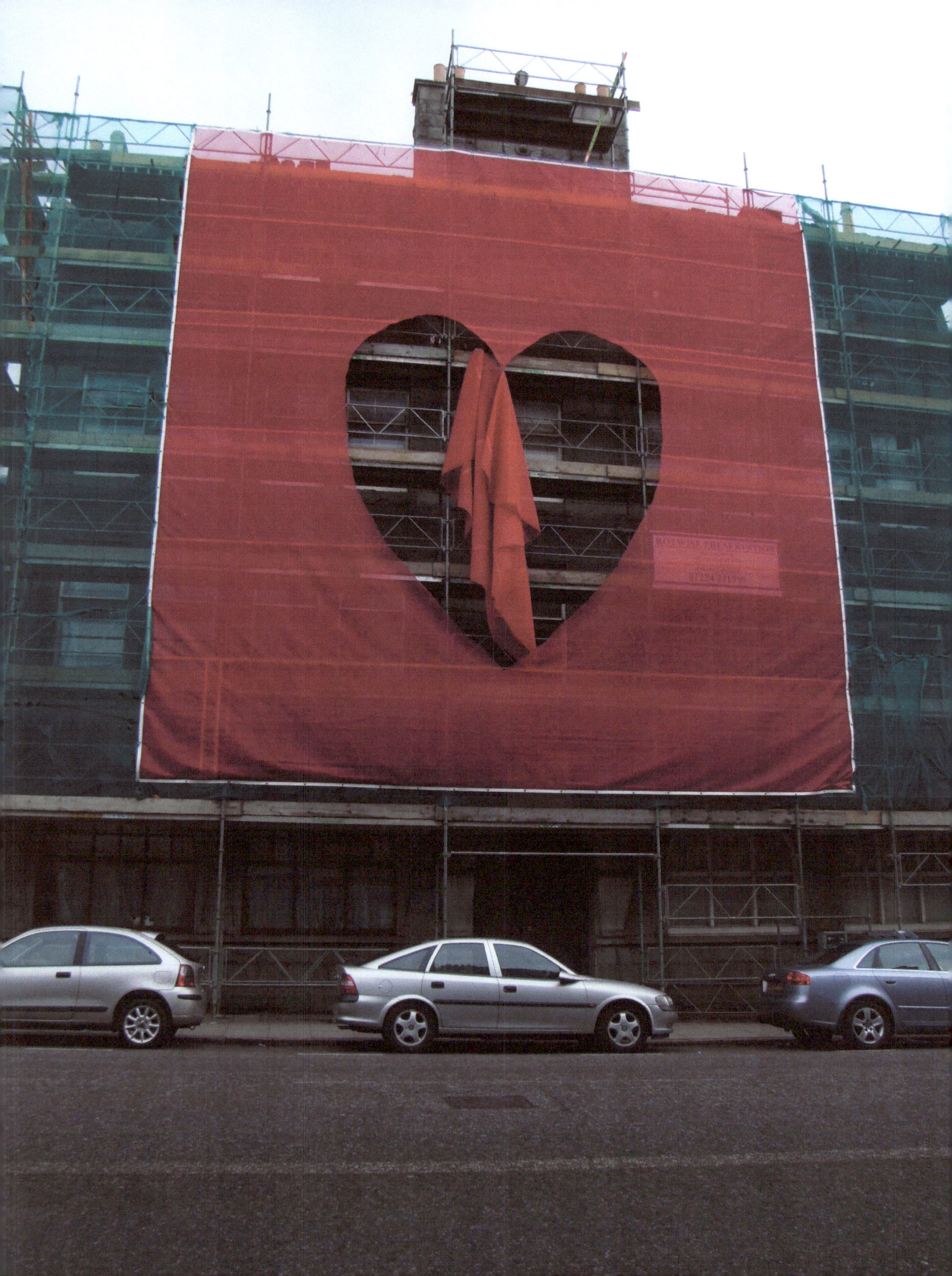

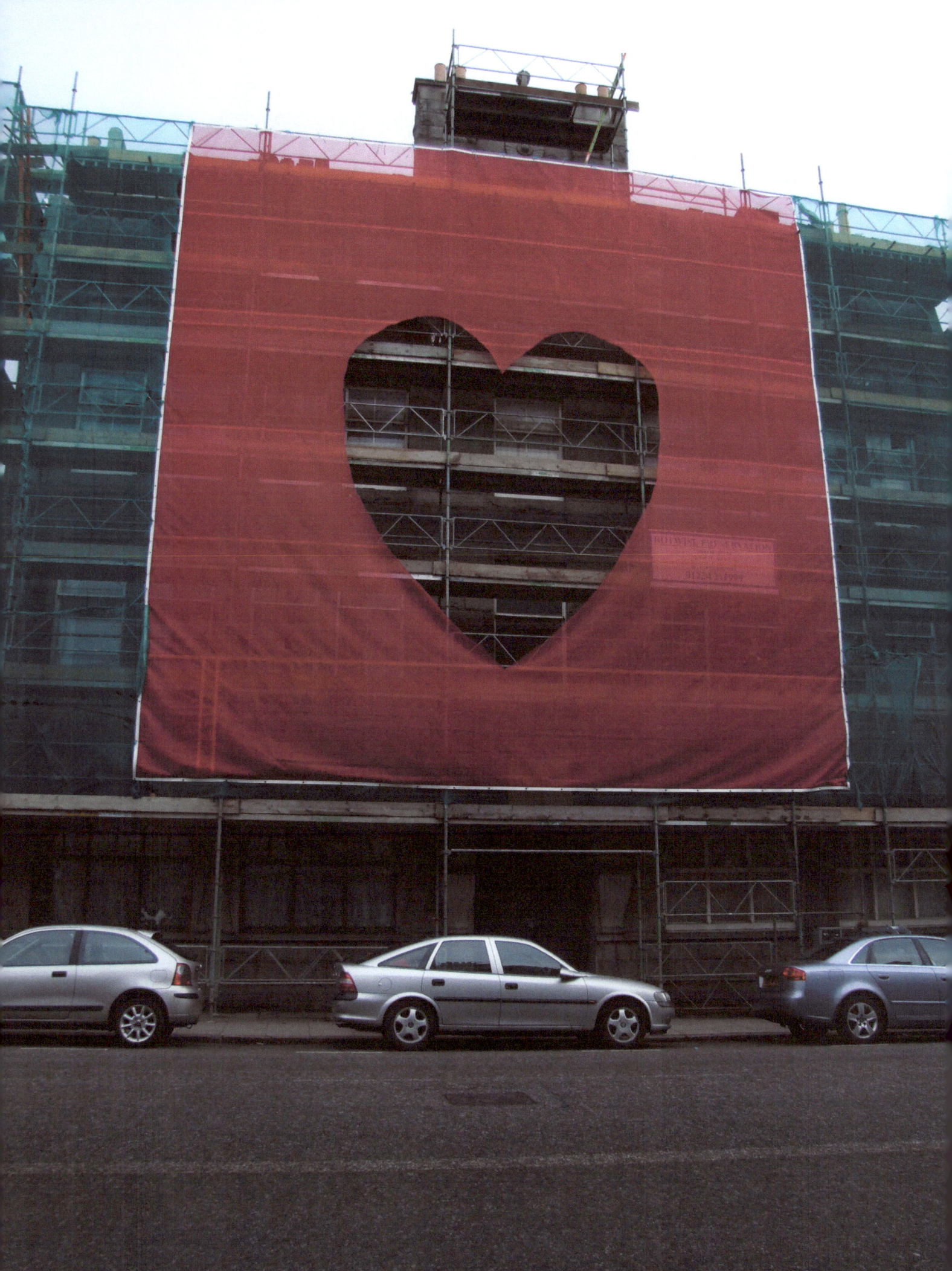

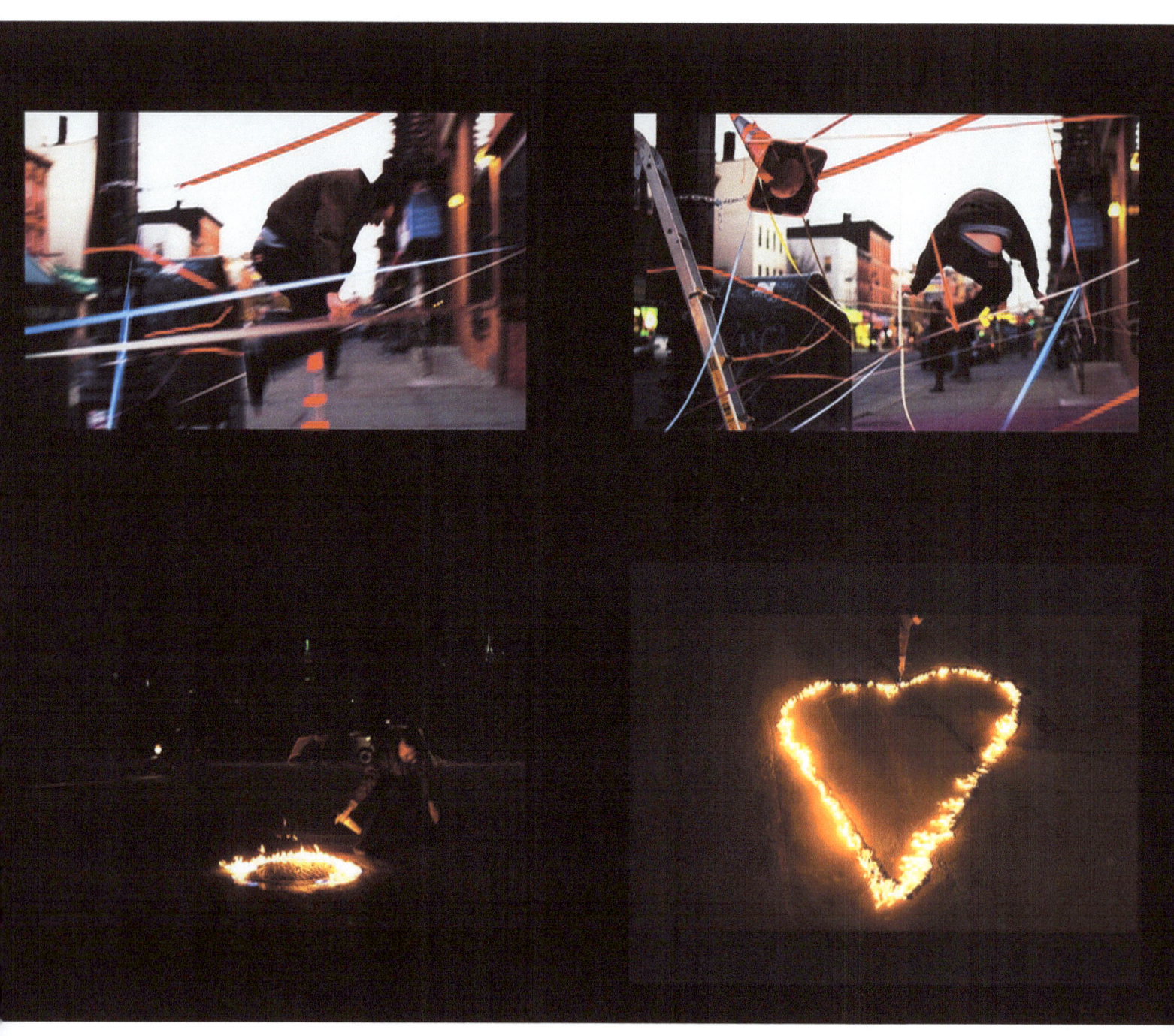

Stills from 'Spontaneous Sculptures' 2007
Location: Brooklyn, New York
7 min 40 sec

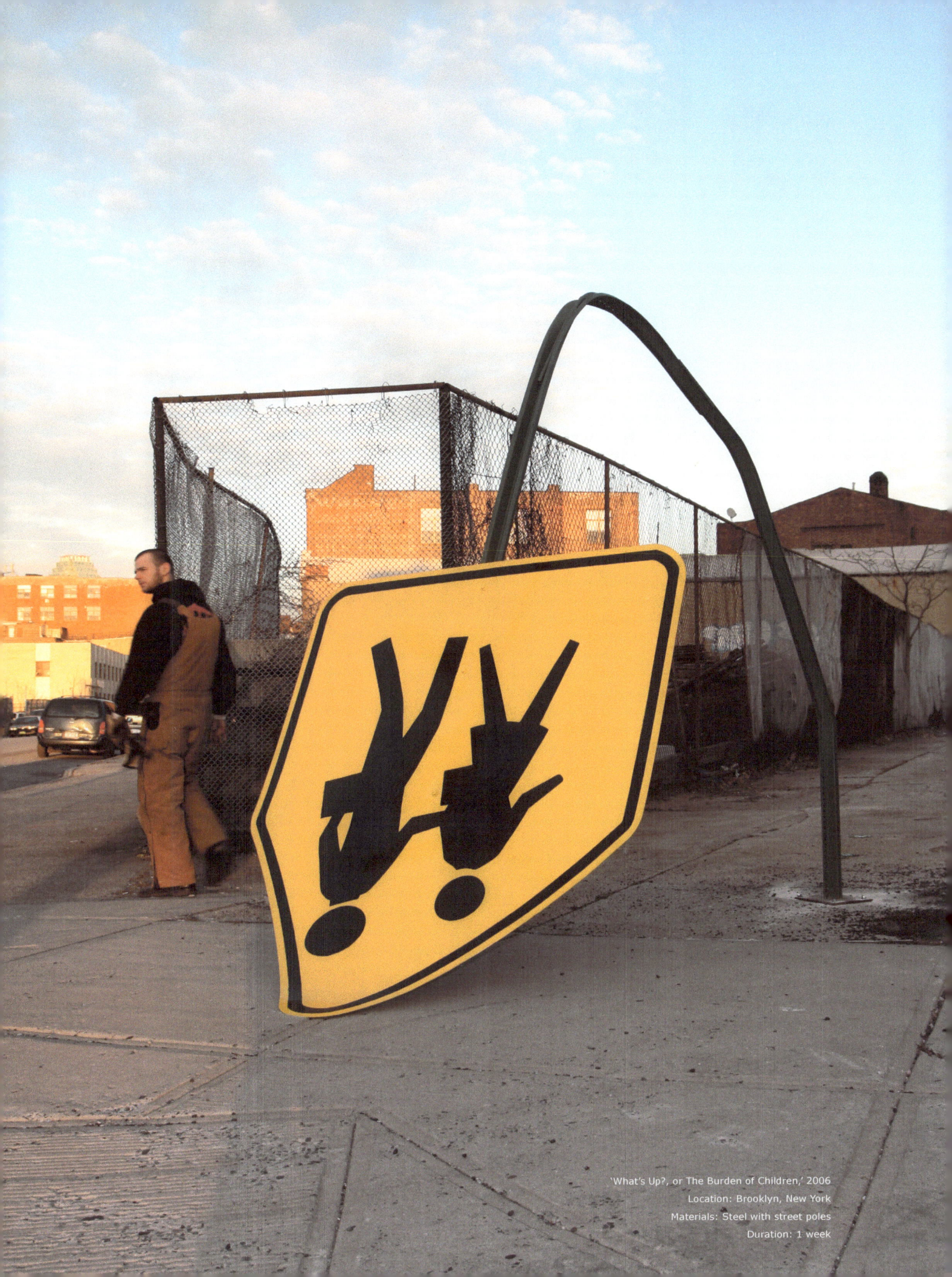

'What's Up?, or The Burden of Children,' 2006
Location: Brooklyn, New York
Materials: Steel with street poles
Duration: 1 week

ULRIKA ERDES

'The basic idea with these public embroideries is to spread a positive feeling, to give people a smile on their lips. But there are also more profound ideas. The Swedish government talks about public space as having three main purposes; meeting, market and movement. This considered it is quite ironic to criminalize people's attempts to meetings and movement. To celebrate the freedom of speech and at the same time trying to restrict people's spontaneous ways of communication is paradoxical. [...] Streetarts flourish where people move and communicate directly with them. The legal aspects can't be ignored. Most street artists work anonymously. To me it is instead important to be open with that it is I who has embroidered on the seats. To show that I believe in this. That I do think it's important we all take responsibility for our common living-room. Because the common, public, is really just that – common. Some say street-art and perhaps graffiti in particular, are ugly and don't demand aesthetic knowledge. But who is really to decide what is pretty or ugly? Good or bad? Shall we legislate about that there should be no bad shoe-makers?

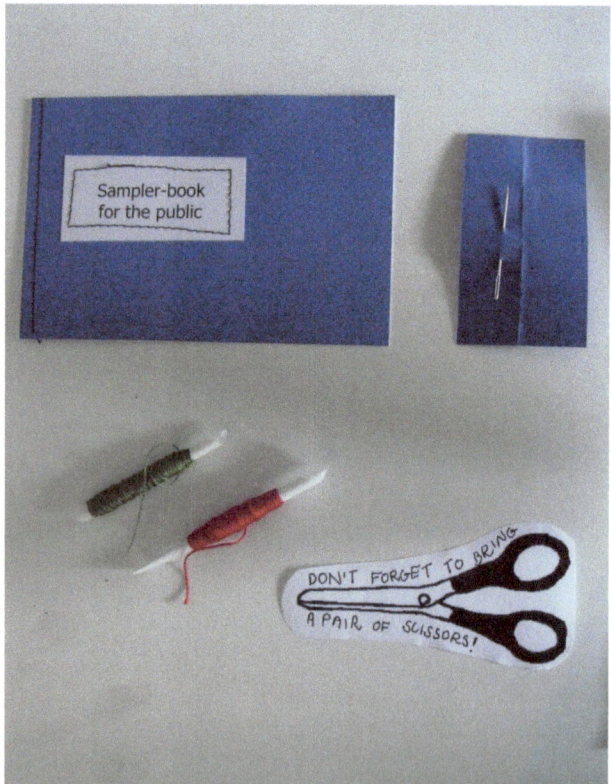

Plan where you sit down. Easiest for right-handed, is to embroider at the seat by your right leg. Make sure you have plenty of time the first time. To fasten the thread: put the needle up an inch or so away from the last stitch. Pull the thread so it's stretched and cut it close to the fabric. The end of the thread will now slip back into the cushion. Please send me photos of your work! [www.ulrikaerdes.se]

[Ulrika Erdes]

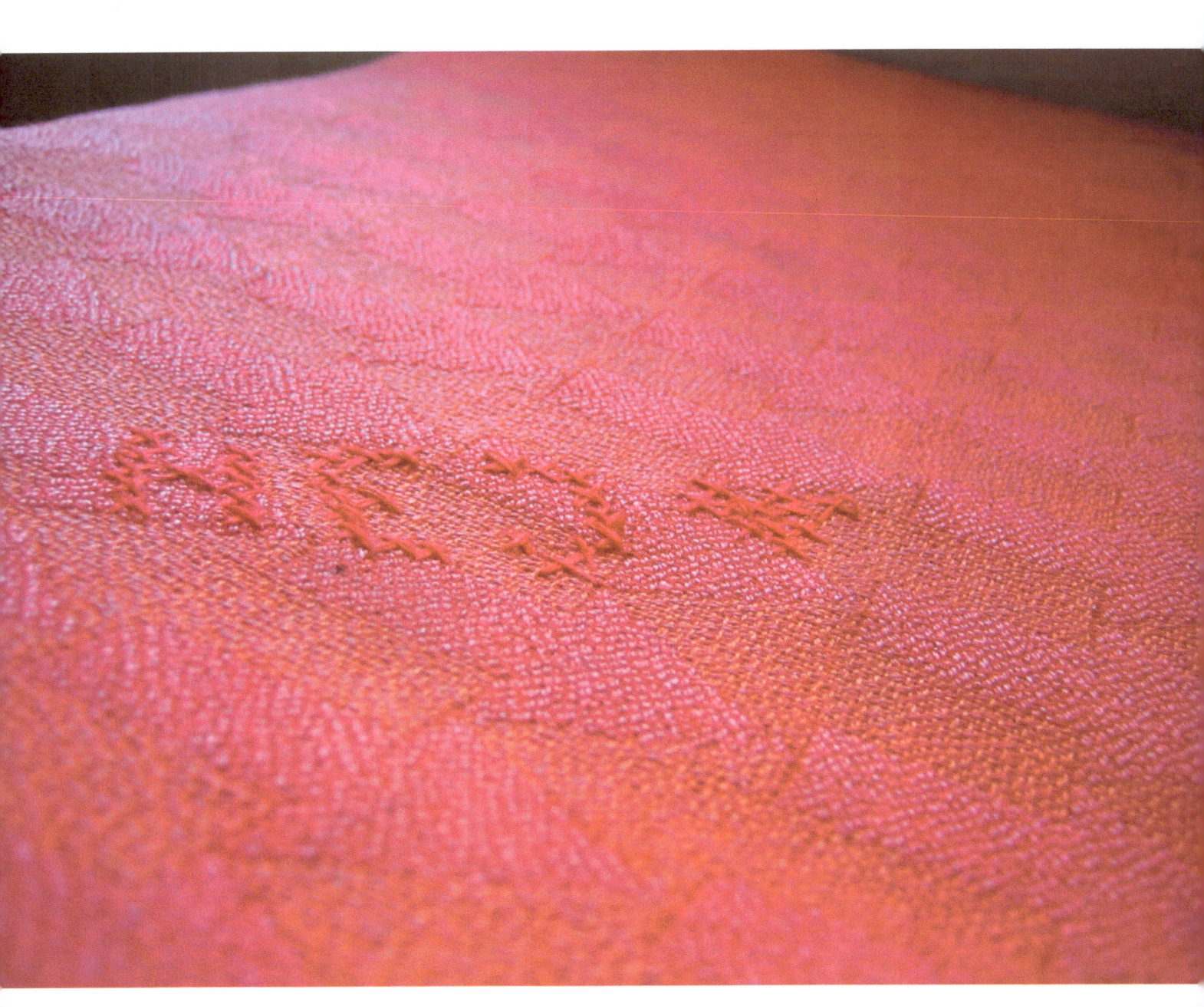

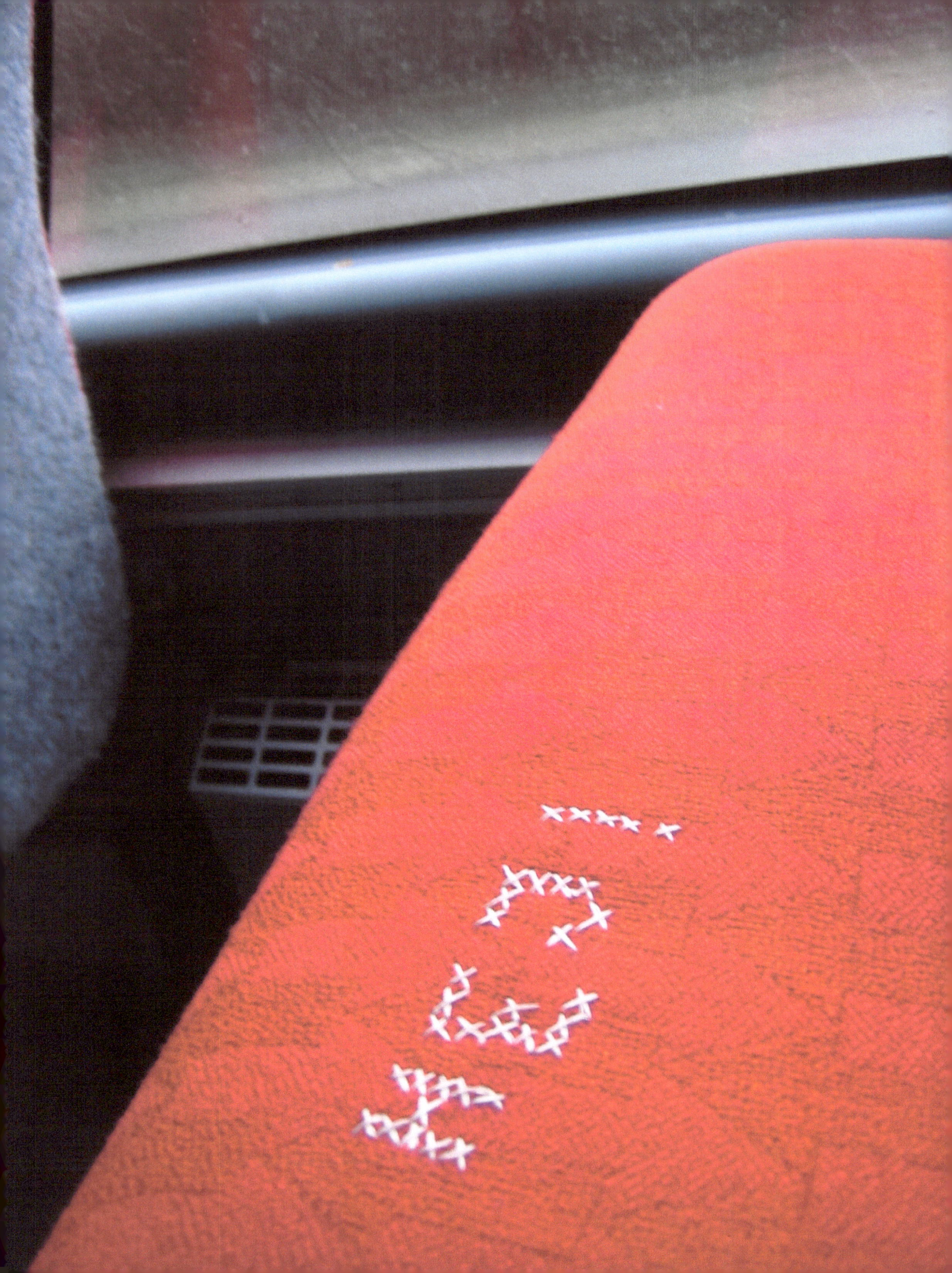

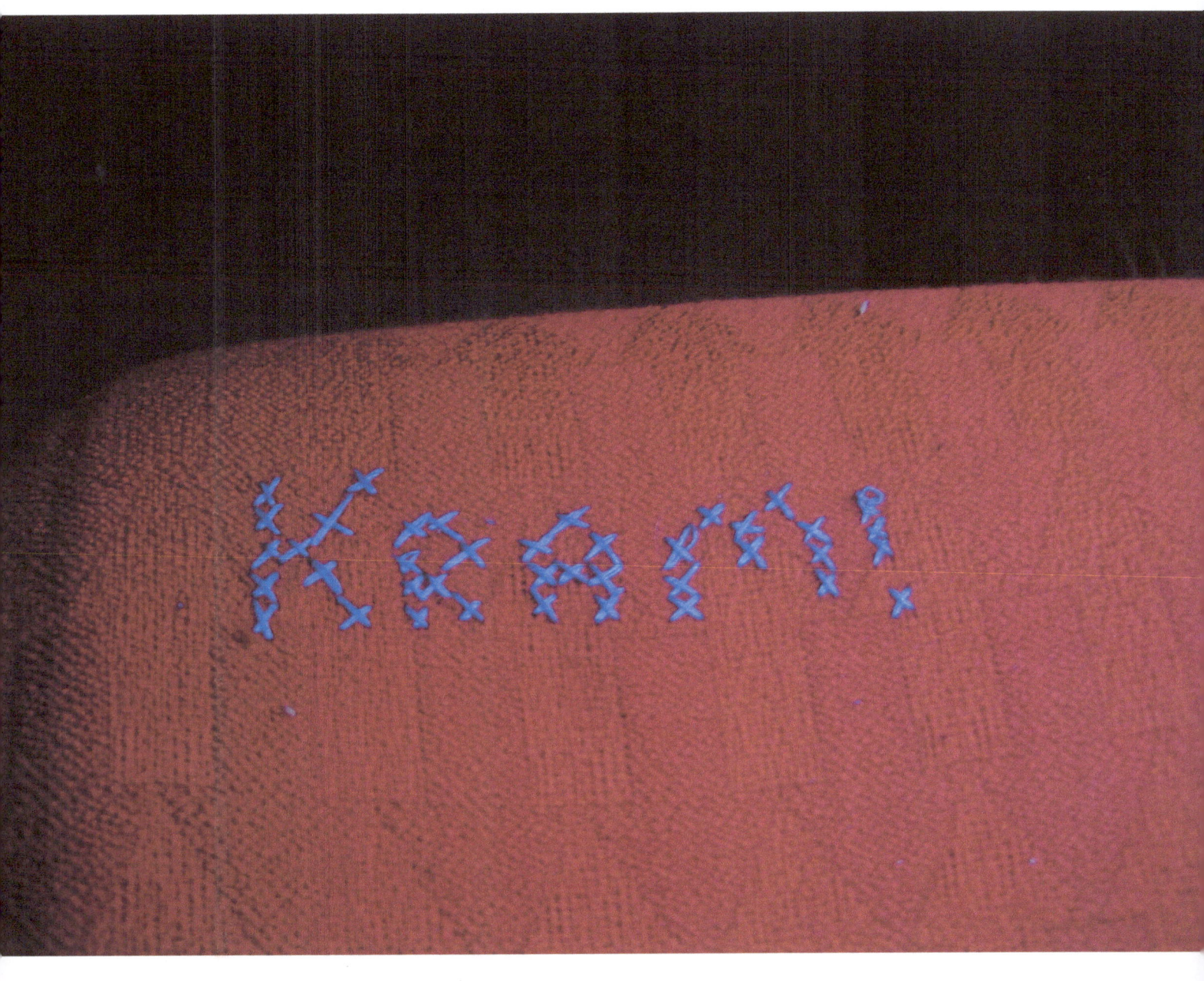

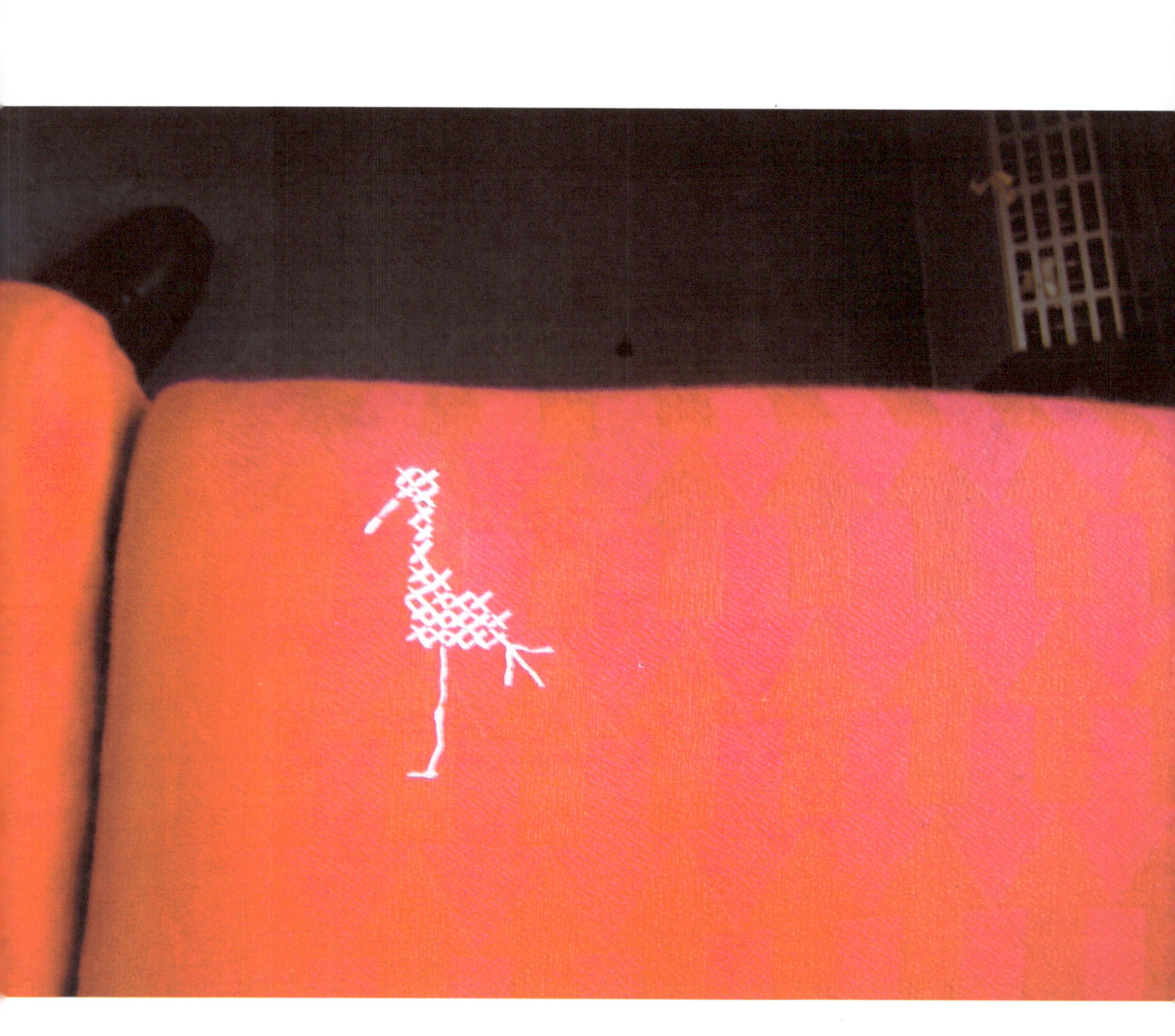

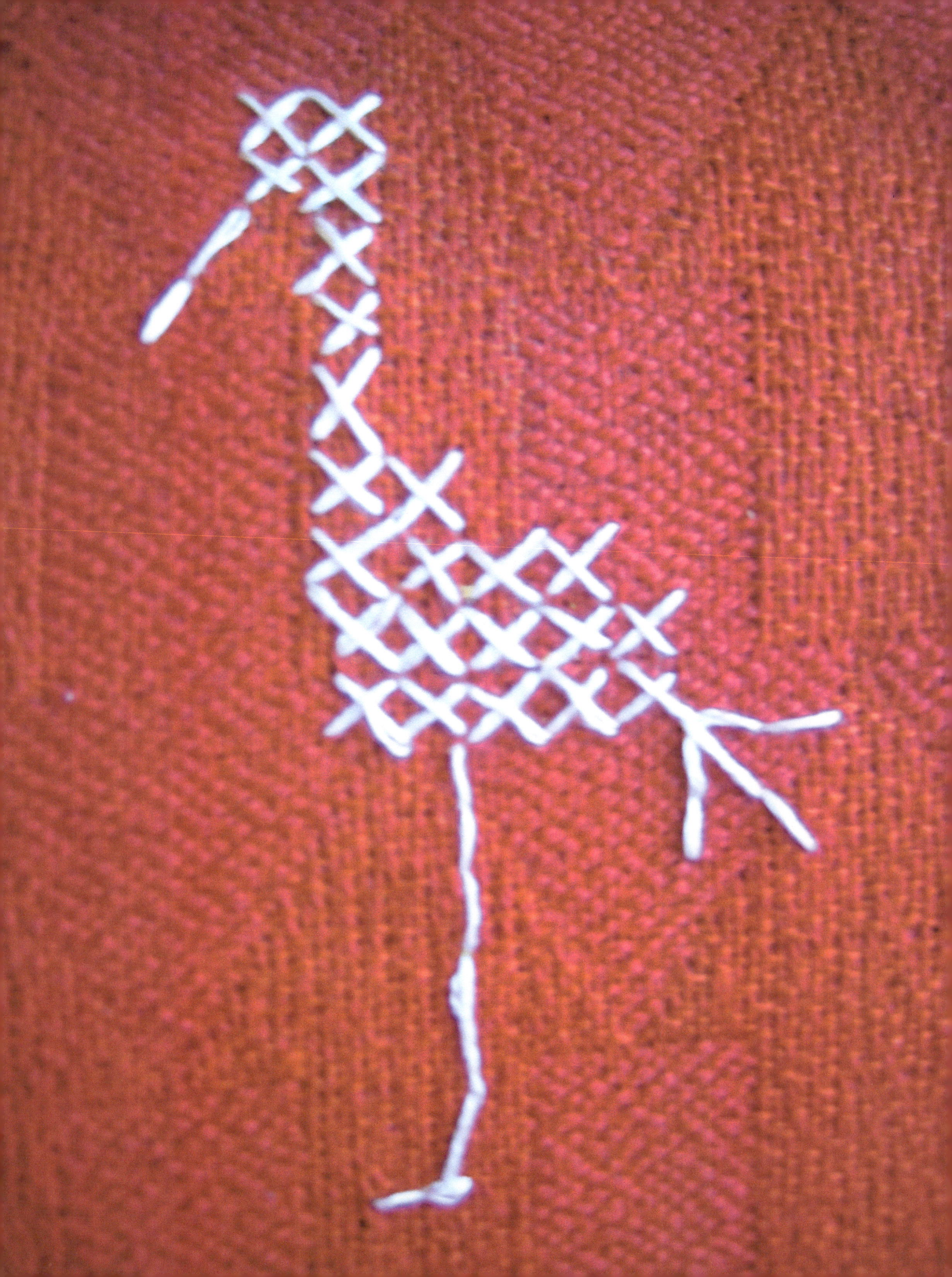

DOMINIC HISLOP

ALL ITEMS OF VALUE
HAVE BEEN REMOVED

Intrigued by the decline in the number of local independent
retailers and growing monocultural dominance of large national
chainstores and supermarket giants in Aberdeen's streets
and market stalls, I documented some visual impressions of
the shifts in urban retail and discussed the impact of changes
with surviving shopkeepers and knowledgeable locals. The
information and images gathered could be viewed as an
installation located in the shopfront of an empty television
repair shop on King Street. Projected photographic images
of some of the numerous empty shops and market stalls in
Aberdeen's city centre, that are in sharp contrast to the sterile
banality of the chainstore design, were projected alongside text
excerpts from interviews made with local independent retailers,
who comment on their position within the shifts and changes
that have taken place within
retail in Aberdeen.

[Dominic Hislop]

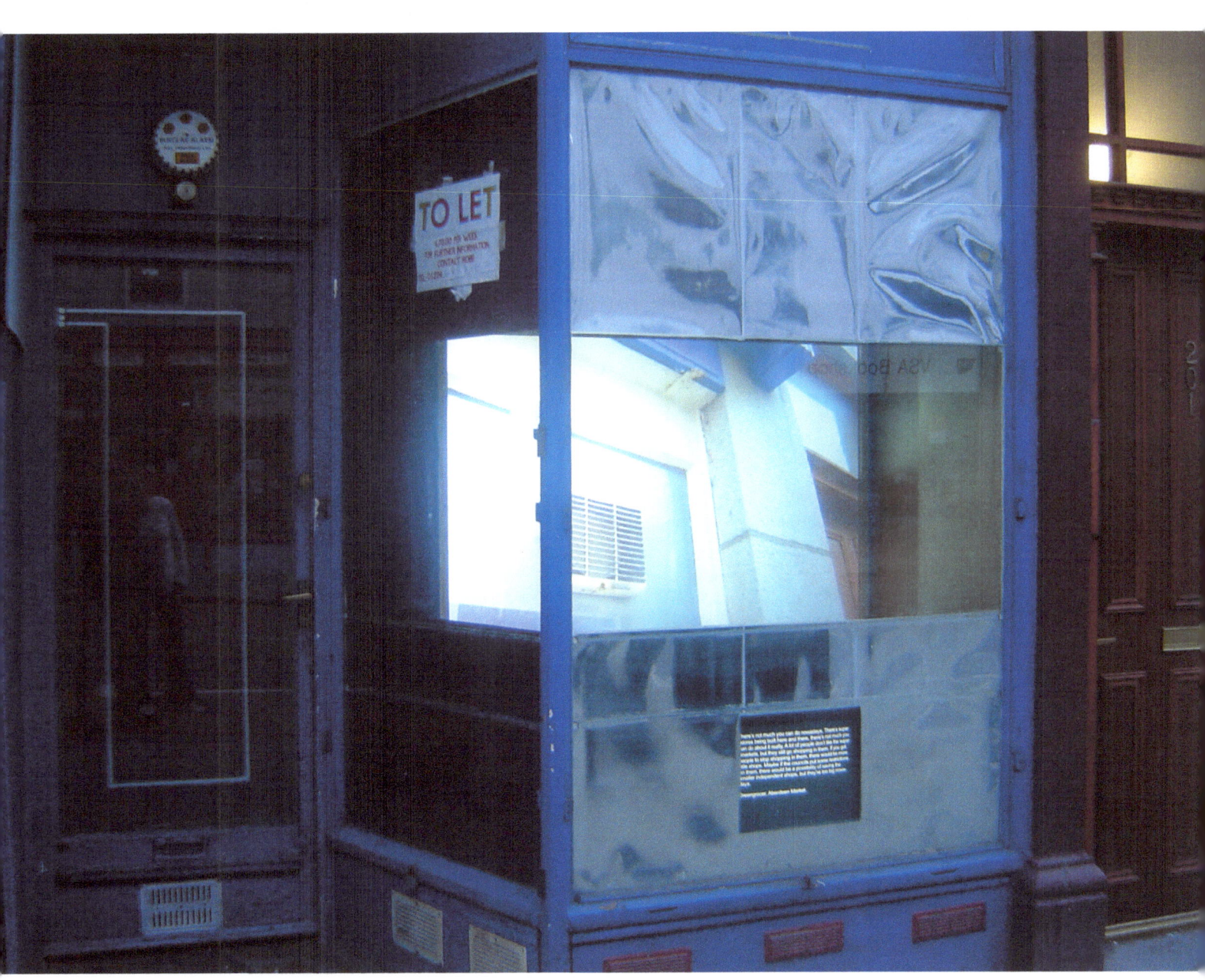

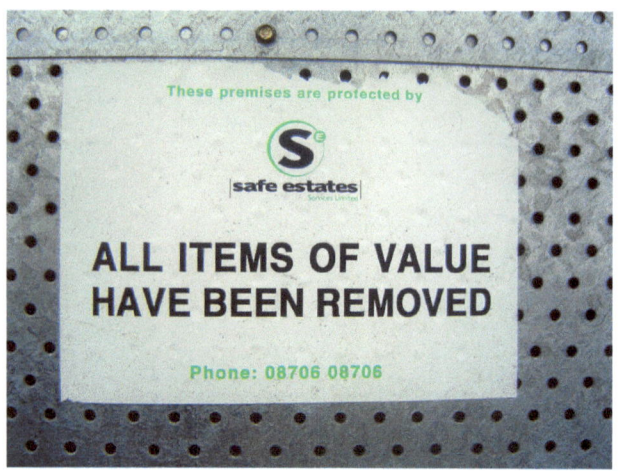

and chemist's. They've all gone. The supermarket in this area has been the cause of every business in this street closing down. Since they've had a café, the Gordon café's business has been slashed by 50%. They've been open 57 years and they're closing next week. The fabric of the community is being destroyed. When they started doing dry cleaning, the dry cleaners closed. Me too. We're now up for sale. Local businesses just can't compete. I could actually at some periods of time be cheaper buying my milk from the supermarket than buying my milk from the supplier, but you name any product and that's the case.

[Convenience store owner, King Street]

Back years ago, the Green used to be absolutely packed full of stalls selling fruit and veg, fish, flowers, you name it, it was here. We're about the only ones left. Not a lot of people appreciate the quality of what was here. There was a lot of homemade, locally grown produce - all within 10 miles from here – using traditional farming methods. I think if you know it's grown locally, it's grown well. The big supermarkets like Tesco and Asda have taken away a lot of the trade. People just see the cheap prices, but most of their stuff is imported and it's obviously not the best quality. Our customers are mostly older people who're used to shopping down here from when it was full of stalls, it might cost a bit more, but I think that as word of mouth spreads that there's more quality stuff here than in supermarkets, we'll manage to keep going.

[Flower and vegetable stallholder, Aberdeen Green]

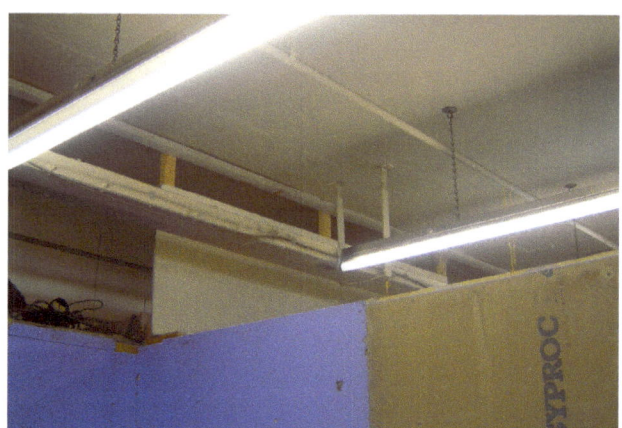

The council in Aberdeen only cares about the big centres like the Bon Accord, St Nicholas and the new Guild Centre that's going to be built down by the train station. When it comes to the side streets, the Aberdeen council doesn't go near them. George Street used to be one big street of independent shops, but that got killed off when they built the Bon Accord and St Nicholas Centre. It's all empty shops and charity shops now. They couldn't give two hoots about the independent retailers.

[Shopkeeper, Castlegate]

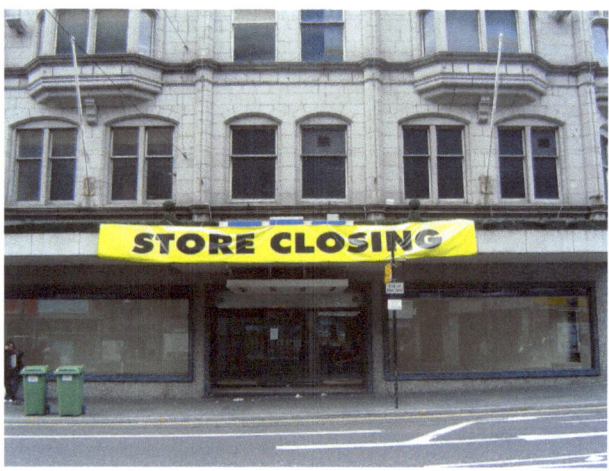

I was born and brought up on this street. 25 years ago, when Safeways (now Morrisons) moved in, from Union Street to the Pittodrie Bar, there were 5 butcher's, 4 baker's, 2 fish shops, 2 fruiterer's, a greengrocer's, a dry cleaner's,

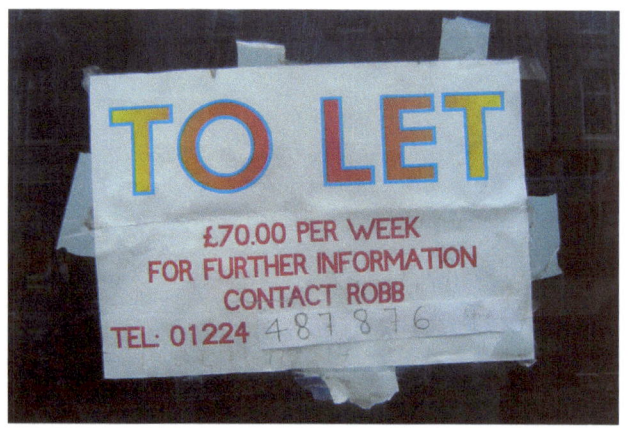

There's been empty shops round here for a few years. Maybe it's something to do with the big shopping centres taking away the heart of the city. Union Street, especially, was a very thriving place. Times have changed. Women didn't use to work, so they had time to go to the shops. Everybody's busy these days and everybody has a car, so they're going out to the suburbs to the big stores where they can get everything cheap and under one roof. I think the quality suffers though. The supermarkets have in-store bakeries, but I don't think they've quite mastered the art of baking. I would like to think that there'll always be a place for a local bakery, but there have been a lot of smaller bakers that have had to close down. We don't make bread anymore. It's no longer profitable, because the super markets make that so cheaply now.

[Baker, George Street]

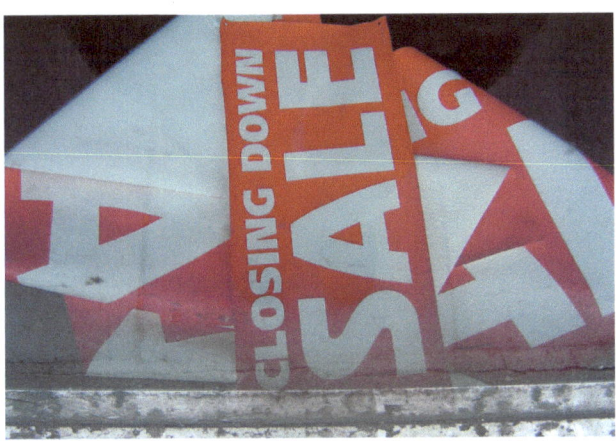

People come from locally and from all over Aberdeen to buy our halal meat. We also have a lot of specialist Asian products. Supermarkets don't stock these kind of things, so we're doing OK.

[Halal meat and grocery shop owner, King Street]

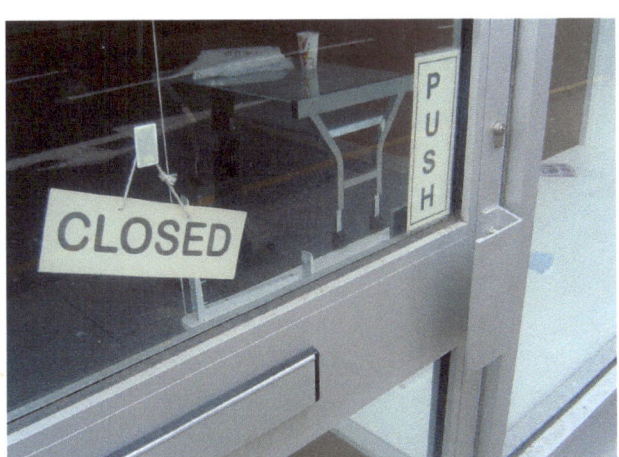

I like to try to do everything as local as I can, but I get a good lot from the Glasgow market. The supermarkets get their goods from all over the world. They can get food all year round, not just seasonal, but a lot of people think the food's better and fresher here than in the supermarkets. I suppose we have different customers to what they get in the supermarkets. A lot of older people come in here. Going to the super markets is too much hassle. Everything's prepacked, they don't want 6 of this or 4 of that, a lot want one. Maybe they're more used to this. A lot of the younger ones, they just go to the supermarkets and do one big shop and get everything in the one place.

[Greengrocer, Aberdeen Market]

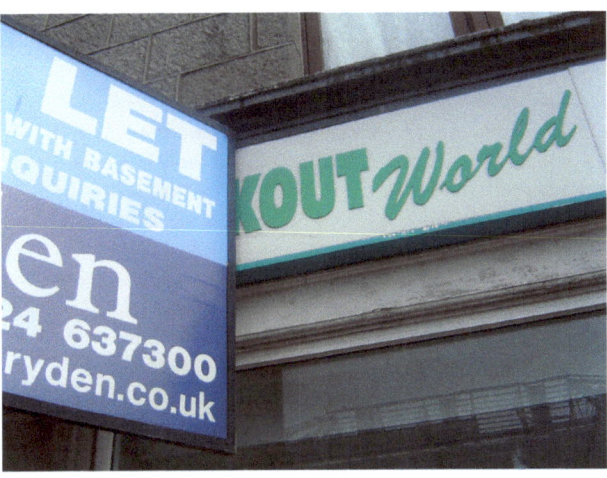

There's not much you can do nowadays. There's super -stores being built here and there, there's not much you can do about it really. A lot of people don't like the super -markets, but they still go shopping in them. If you got people to stop shopping in them, there would be more little shops. Maybe if the councils put some restrictions on them, there would be a possibility of saving the smaller independent shops, but they're too big nowadays.

[Greengrocer, Aberdeen Market]

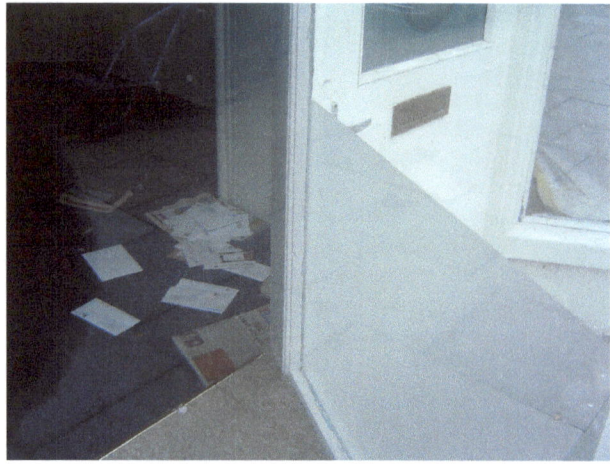

they want and we've destroyed our local economy, I don't think they'll really like the consequences. People in Western countries are just massive consumers. We don't produce anything anymore. This country is only shuffling paper... electronically. So, what happens when the Third World countries on whose backs all of this is possible say, 'We want some of your standard of living.' What happens when they get organized and knowledgeable enough to put their prices up? What's going to happen then, cos we won't have any alternative local produce anymore? How do we start producing again? There's no way back.

[Convenience store owner, King Street]

All up Union Street, much of the products are made in China or the Far East. We're now holding down our cost of living by virtue of cheap goods and that diminishes our ability to produce, distribute and retail. When the prices inevitably go up, the cost of living will suddenly rise and we will not have the means to match that outlay. Governments have to be foresighted and keep some basic manufacturing in this country. If we become a nation of facilitators and service providers, we're totally at the mercy of people from outside. We tend to think that after World War II everything is going to be jolly, that there's not going to be any more wars and bombs and we're going to keep the hordes at bay, but it just isn't so. Cultures go down, empires crumble and I think the demise of the shop is evidence of this.

[Retired Doctor, Aberdeen]

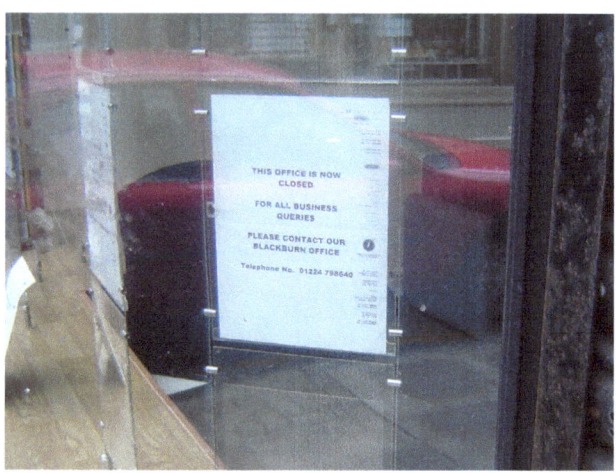

There's no more manufacturing in this country anymore. It's all made in China or in third world countries with cheap parts and labour. So, if a vacuum cleaner or iron or whatever breaks down, in the past I could repair it, but mostly now there's no standards to how it's been made and there's no place to order new parts from. Kettles and irons and these kind of goods are sold so cheaply now at Asda or Tesco's that you're as well just chucking away the old ones and buying a new one. There are mountains of electrical junk. I don't know what the future of this business is. I used to have 3 people working here, now there's only me. If things keep going the way they are, something's going to happen. There'll be some kind of collapse. They can't go on like this.

[Electrical repair shopkeeper, King Street]

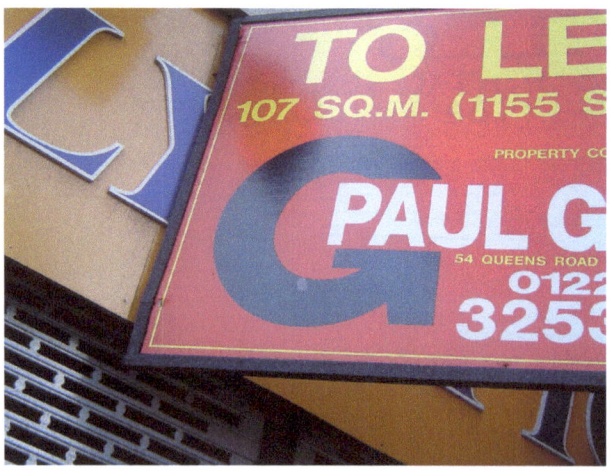

Having said all that, this is what the people want. We want as much of everything as possible as easily and as cheaply as possible. If people didn't shop at supermarkets, it would be different. At the end of the day, when people get what

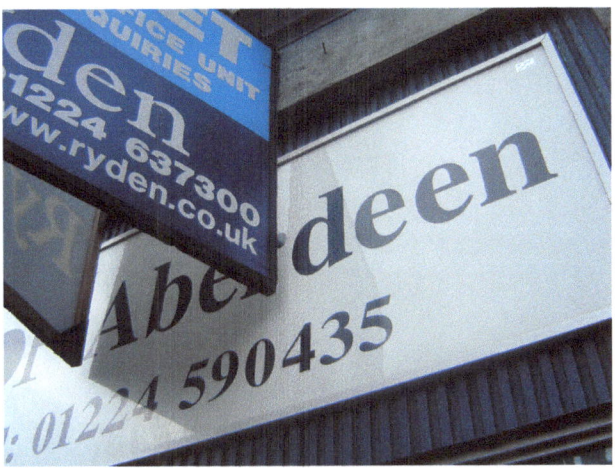

It's what the tourists look for when they come to a city. 'Where's the market?' But there's no market in Aberdeen. I used to have a stall at the Green. The Green was the original market. It was busy years ago, but there's nothing down there now really. It's dead now. Then I had a stall at the Castlegate, which was the main market and a better market. It was a busy 3-day market with about 100 stalls, till the council forced us out. They wanted to make this into a cultural area and said we should go down to the Green. Unfortunately some people wouldn't move. If they'd all moved, there'd have still been a market there. But nobody will go down there now. Aberdeen is a bit snobby, so the local Joe Bloggs market traders have to go down to the Green, but they'll close off Union Street for the posh international market. Is that very fair?

[Former stallholder, Castlegate Market]

King Street's dead now. When I was a teenager, there used to be a couple of cafés over there, a bicycle shop there, a butcher across the road, a baker down the road. We've been here for 57 years, but we're closing next week. They're converting the café into flats. It's just not making enough money anymore. It used to be packed in here. On Saturday mornings there used to be a queue to get in. People would come here when there were more shops in the area. Now they go down to Morrisons to do all their shopping and go into the café there. The smoking ban has affected us badly too. Some of our staff have been here for over 20 years and with E&M's* closing in April, there's a lot of people looking for jobs. There are some jobs out there, but most of these people offer £5.35 an hour, and when you're in your 40s, 50s or 60s, that's just degrading.

[Café worker, King Street]

*E&M's (Esslemont & Macintosh) was a locally owned department store.

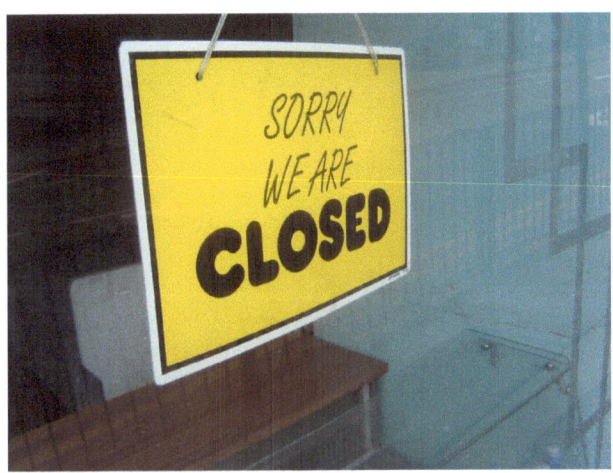

LEOPOLD KESSLER

My interventions in public space are based on changing,
repairing or extending the function or use of public items, like
signs, benches, streetlamps. I usually don´t ask for permission,
so the works become part of urban reality and stay until they
are removed. The interventions are located between selfless
service and selfjustice, an undemocratic taking things in own
hands. From the technical perspective the works are simple. It's
important for me to stay on a level which could be practicable
for everybody. I try to analyse the borders and legitimations
of law. The information about the existence of works or the
way they function is given in exhibitions and then spreads as a
rumour in the city.

[Leopold Kessler]

birdhouses/nyc, 2005
Still from video
lombard&freid projects

When I walked through Greenwich Village I noticed that there
are birdhouses in the trees, installed by the people who are
living there. I found that interesting as a sign of individual
realisation in this somehow very paranoid and hot public
space of New York, especially with the alcohol prohibition. I
manufactured ten birdhouses, all containing liquor, all with
different clues how to get the alcohol. Five of them I installed
in public space, five in the gallery, where people could also use
them. Then there was a map of the location of the 'outside-
houses' and a video showing one guy strolling through New
York, drinking out of birdhouses, matching with the life around
- baseball game in Brooklyn, joggers in Hudson River Park etc.

privatised, Paris, 2001-03
Stills from video
galerie corentin hamel

I installed receivers in eight street lamps which enable me to
switch the lamps on/off by remote control. I'm trying to sell
those to people who are either interested in art or street lamps
or believe in personal responsibility.

Import Budapest-Vienna, 2006
Stills from video
A package of cigarettes is stuck on a train, departing from
Budapest. I was waiting at the train station in Vienna. The
package 'arrives' in front of me, I collect the package, light one
cigarette and leave. We repeated it six times.

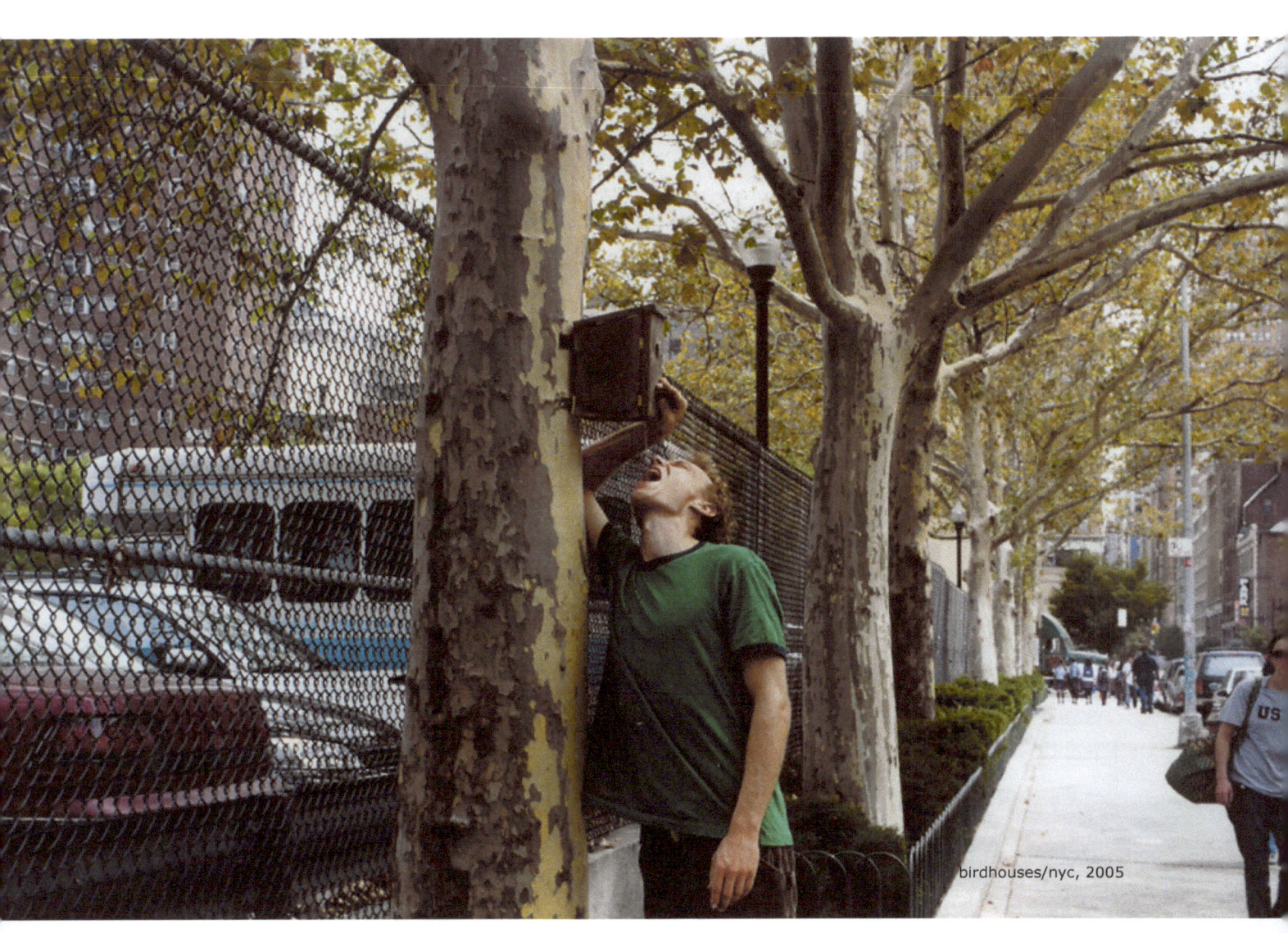

birdhouses/nyc, 2005

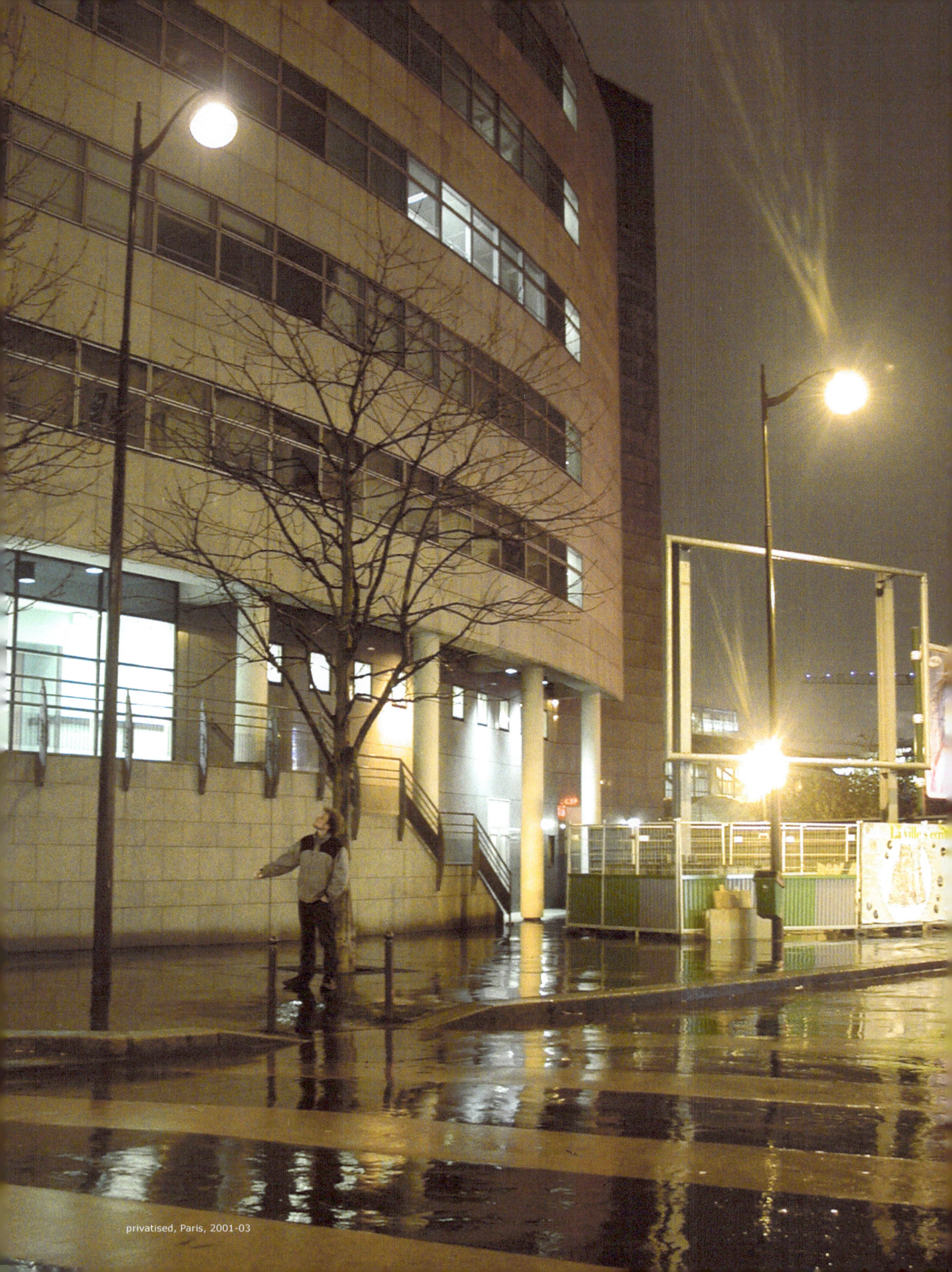

privatised, Paris, 2001-03

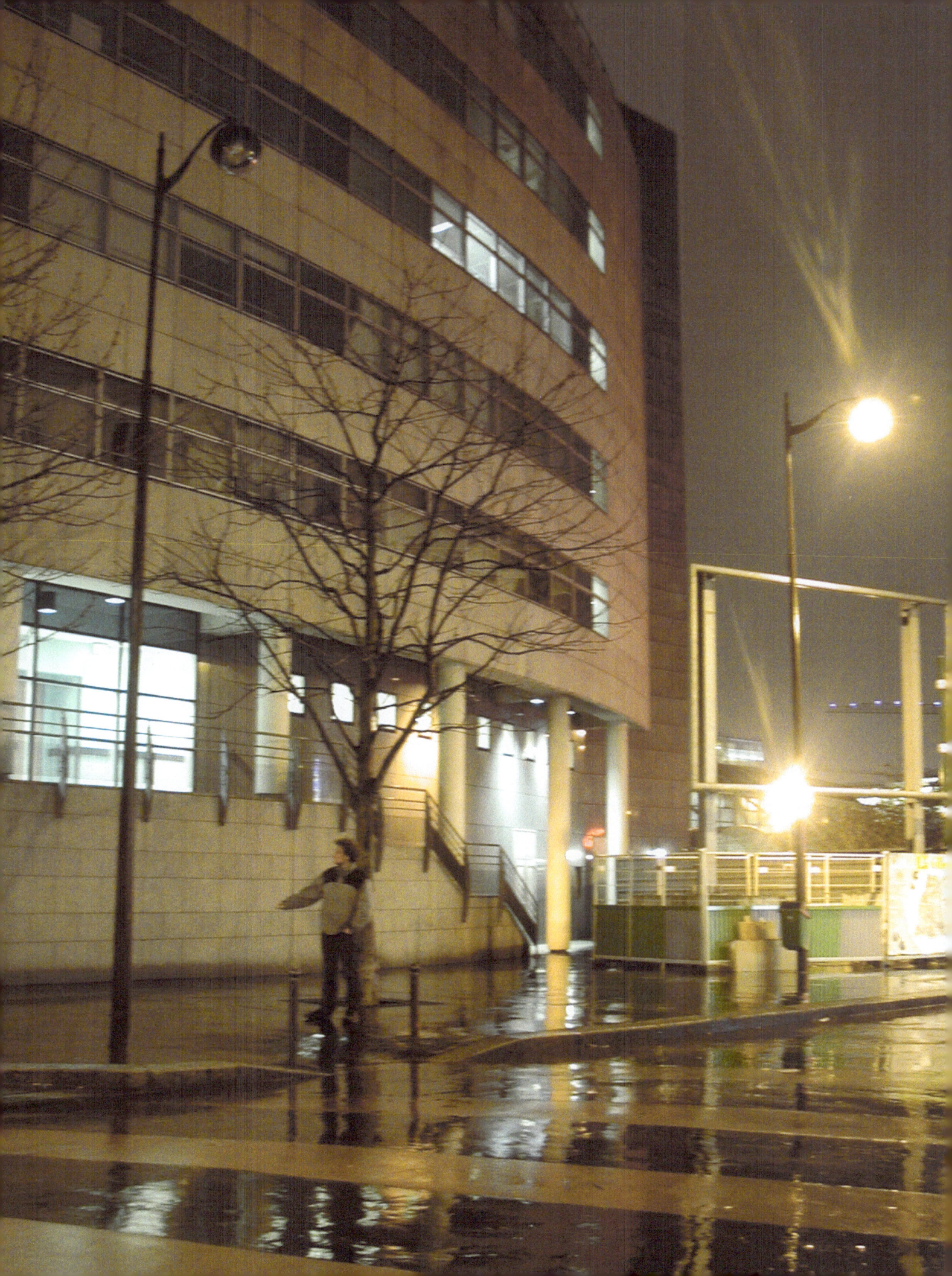

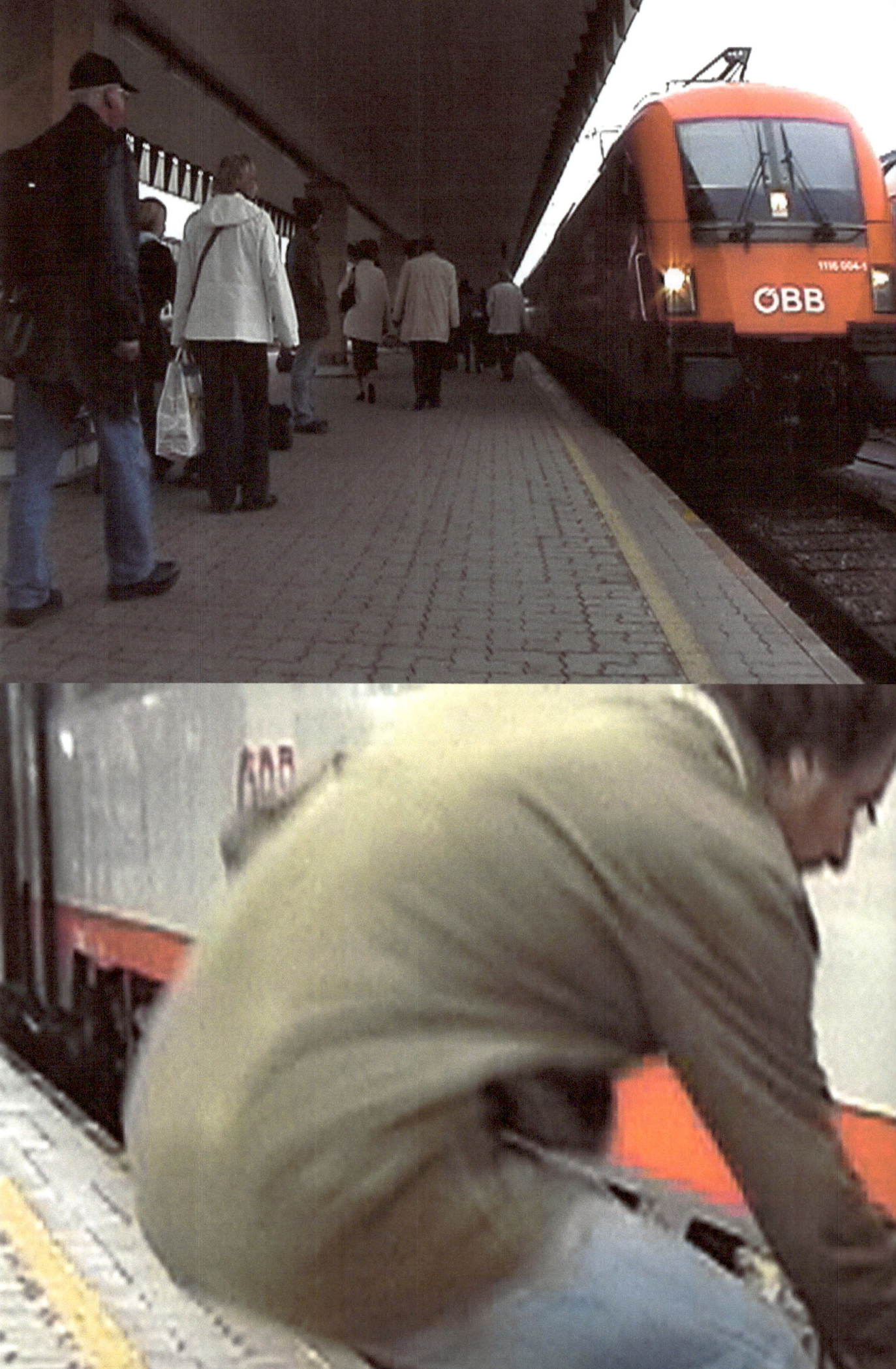

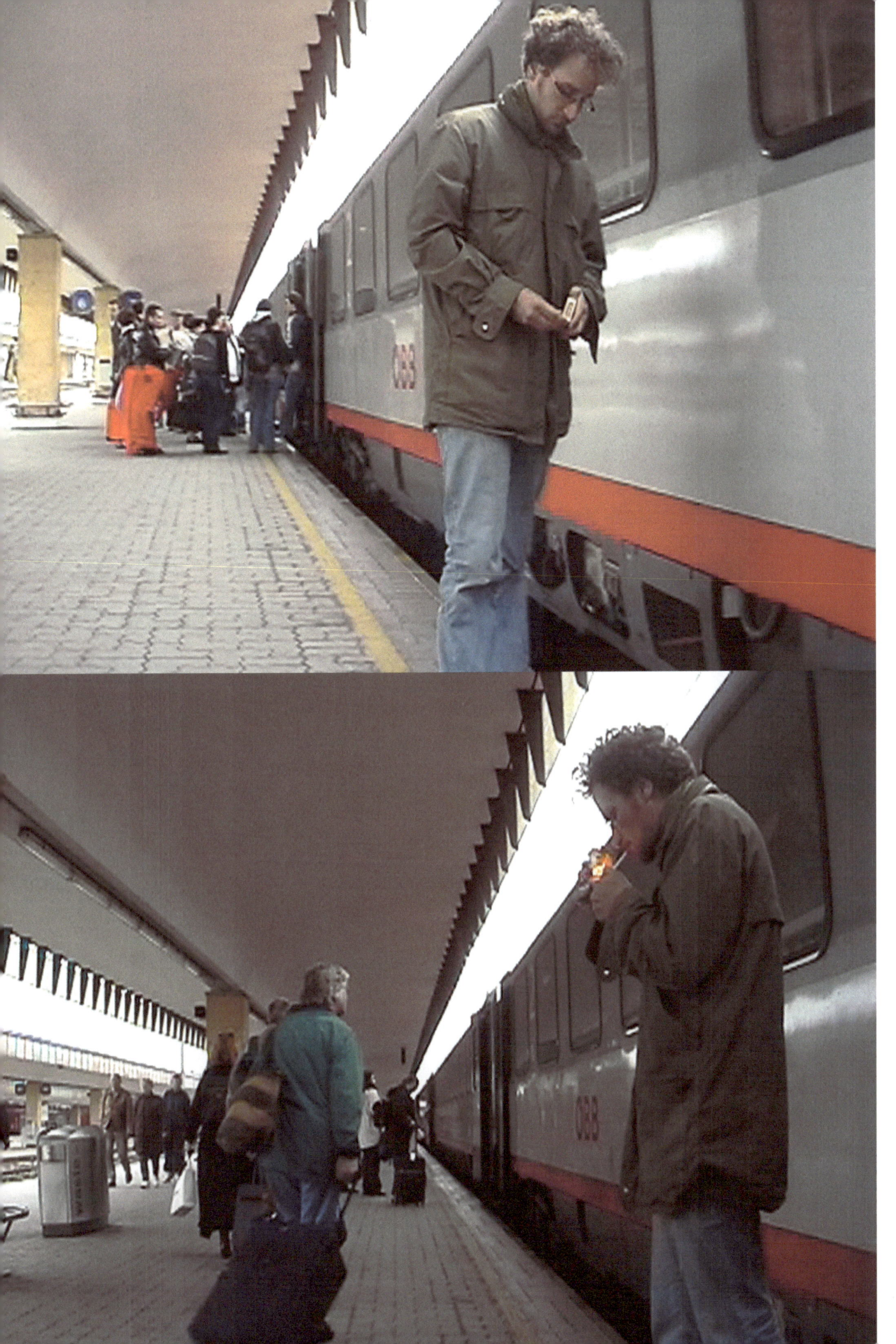

CONTRIBUTORS

ADAMS lives in Copenhagen. He works in public space without permission. Over the years his work has come to be more and more hidden. His most recent projects are site-specific clandestine constructions in the streets and beneath.

AKAY, KIDPELE and MADE - aka APA - work together in Stockholm. Their ideas are silly, their work is site-specific, and their documentation is always very serious.

GILES BAILEY is an artist who lives and works in Glasgow. He initiated the independent music collective Nuts and Seeds and is a committee member of Transmission Gallery.

BRETT BLOOM and BONNIE FORTUNE live in Chicago. Brett is an artist, writer and organizer. He works with the group Temporary Services and is a founding member of the experimental cultural centre in Chicago called Mess Hall. Bonnie Fortune is an artist. She investigates place and social relationships through walking, photography and booklet making. She is the founding member of Free Walking, a framework for peripatetic investigations of Chicago and the surrounding areas. Brett and Bonnie collaborate on a multi-part project called 'Let's Re-Make the World'. With this title as their programme, they look at radical ideas from the 1970s to create new projects and investigations into fomenting change and remaking the world.

MARJOLIJN DIJKMAN lives in Rotterdam. In 2005 Marjolijn founded together with Maarten Vanden Eynde Enough Room For Space, a mobile platform for site specific cultural projects. For more information see marjolijndijkman.com and enoughroomforspace.org

BRAD DOWNEY studied at the Pratt Art Institute in New York and at the Slade School of Fine Art in London. His work provides a subtle, yet mischievous response to street furniture and signs, and their structuring of public life. As well as (illicit) sculptures in public space, Brad Downey makes films about actions in the street. His documentary film 'Public Discourse' (2003) documents the practice of a diverse range of artists who make work in public space without permission. As described by journalist Tamara Warren 'he approaches his work with a common thread designed to engage spectators as social critics.'

ULRIKA ERDES, born in Landvetter, Sweden, studied cultural sciences in Linköping. She is currently studying painting in Malmö and creates performances and paintings.

DOMINIC HISLOP, born in Dumfries, Scotland and grown up a bit in Cardenden, Fife but mostly in Edinburgh, lives in Berlin. He also works together with artists Miklos Erhardt, and more recently Elske Rosenfeld as Big Hope, focused on engaging with social issues and communicating with a broader public in art.

LEOPOLD KESSLER, born in Munich, lives and works in Vienna. He studied at the Academies of Fine Arts in Munich and later Vienna.

JULIE PEETERS lives and works in Gent, Belgium.

BRIAN ROSS studied at Gray's School of Art, Aberdeen. He creates intricate, large scale free-hand drawings in marker pen and recently painted two public murals in Aberdeen, one inside the Transition Extreme Sports Centre, and a second on the main doors of Limousine Bull Gallery.

ADAPTATION
Redesigning the everyday.

Presented by Peacock Visual Arts for Six Cities Design Festival.
05 May-16 June 2007

Peacock Visual Arts
21 Castle Street
Aberdeen AB11 5BQ
peacockvisualarts.com

Published by Peacock Visual Arts, Aberdeen, Scotland
Editor | Monika Vykoukal
Essay | Giles Bailey
Photographs | The Artists, Peacock Visual Arts,
The Vacuum Cleaner, Craig Barrowman, Brian Ross
Design | Scott Masser

ISBN 978 0 9543574 9 8

Peacock Visual Arts Team
Director | Lindsay Gordon
Curator | Monika Vykoukal
Assistant Curator | Angela Lennon
Press and Marketing | Nina Eggens
Printmaking | Michael Waight, Linsay Croall
Digital | Adam Proctor
Digital Assistant | Dawn Ford
3sixty-tv | Jack Keenan
Darkroom Technician | Nicole Plumb
Framing | David McCracken, Mark McCracken
Gallery Assistant | Dana Swanson
Accounts | Alison Kennedy
Factota | Sandy Simpson and Douglas Colvin

Interns | Gaëlle Masselot, Robin Sudbury

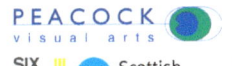
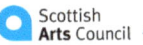

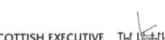